Excel

ADVANCED SKILLS

ENGLISH

YEAR 6

AGES 11–12

WRITING WORKBOOK

Get the Results You Want!

PASCAL PRESS

Laura Anderson

Reprinted 2018, 2019, 2021, 2023, 2024

ISBN 978 1 74125 406 8

Pascal Press
PO Box 250
Glebe NSW 2037
(02) 9198 1748
www.pascalpress.com.au

Publisher: Vivienne Joannou
Project editors: Rosemary Peers and Mark Dixon
Edited and proofread by Michael Wyatt
Answers checked by Glenda Walsh
Series developer: Laura Anderson
Series consultant: Kristine Brown
Cover and page design by DiZign Pty Ltd
Typeset by Kim Webber
Printed by Vivar Printing/Green Giant Press

Contents

To the student

This book will help you with your writing tasks, in English and in other subjects.

There are nine units altogether, each focusing on a different type of text. Some texts are imaginative, such as narratives and poems. Others are factual, such as reports and explanations.

Each unit contains an introduction that explains the purpose of the text and its special features. There are also examples of students' first drafts. These are followed by practice exercises that aim to improve the draft. Some of the exercises focus on the structure of the text. Others focus on its language features. There is one example of a student's final draft. Make sure you read it carefully and answer the questions beside each paragraph.

At the end of the unit is a text in which words, sentences or paragraphs are missing. You should try to fill in the missing sections, using the step-by-step improvement exercises to help you. In the final activity, you are given a list of topics and you have to choose one to write about.

Most of the activities can be written in this book, but you will have to use your own paper for the final writing activity. I suggest you buy a notebook or folder for this. If you are not sure how to write something, use the sample texts and the checklists to help you.

It is best to work through the book from Unit 1 to the end. This will help you build on skills you have already learned. However, if you are learning about a particular type of text in school, you could do that unit in the book. For example, if you are learning about explanations, you could do Unit 5.

It is important that you have a dictionary and a thesaurus handy as you work through the book, and that you ask for help if you need it. There is also a list of useful vocabulary at the end of the book to help you with your writing.

I hope you enjoy reading the texts and doing the activities.

Good luck!

Laura Anderson

About this book

This book consists of nine units, each covering a different type of text. Each unit contains two samples of students' first drafts. These are followed by exercises designed to help the students improve their drafts. There is one example of a final draft, which models the text for students. Students are then asked to complete a partially constructed final draft, and finally to construct a text independently. These last two activities allow students to put the knowledge they have acquired into practice.

The units are organised as follows:

An introduction to the text

This page looks at the features of the text. There are also short exercises to help students identify the type of text or its features.

Student A: Writing the first draft

These two pages focus on the planning and writing of the first draft. There is a comprehensive checklist that enables students to identify the features that have or have not been included in the draft, as well as other short exercises.

A step-by-step improvement plan

This section contains four steps designed to help students improve the draft. Some of the steps focus on the structure of the text, while others focus on the language features.

Writing the final draft

The final draft is an example of a more advanced student's writing. It is accompanied by comments that point out the features of the text, as well as questions that ask students to identify some of the features.

Student B: Writing the first draft

The second half of the unit looks at another first draft, followed by a step-by-step improvement plan. Students are then asked to complete a partially constructed final draft.

Your turn

The final page of the unit contains a list of topics, from which students choose one to write about. Included is a checklist to guide students in their writing. There is also a note directing students to a word bank at the back of the book where they can find vocabulary to help them with the writing task.

Word bank

At the end of the book is a word bank where students will find useful lists of words and phrases to help them complete their independent writing tasks.

Unit 1 Factual recounts—newspaper reports

Looking at recounts

A **recount** is generally an **informative** text. It tells about something that has already happened, in the order in which the events took place.

Examples of recounts include diary and journal entries, historical reports, letters, emails and postcards, newspaper reports and biographies or autobiographies. In this unit we will be looking at **newspaper reports**.

The main **purpose** of a newspaper report is to give readers **information** about people and events in an interesting way.

A **newspaper report** should have:

* a **headline** that captures the reader's attention and contains a hint of what the report is about. The headline is usually short and is written in a large, bold font.
* an **orientation**, or introduction, that sets the scene. It tells the reader **who** was involved, **what** happened and **where**, **when** and sometimes **why** the events took place.
* a **retelling** of the events, usually in the order in which they happened.
* **quotes** or **statements** from witnesses or people involved.
* a **final paragraph** that wraps up the report.

1. In each of the following pairs, which is more likely to be a newspaper **headline**?

a Counting Down! ☐

b The final is only two days away ☐

c An earthquake causes a bridge to collapse ☐

d Earthquake destroys bridge ☐

2. Which of the texts below could be the opening paragraph of a **newspaper report**?

a Tropical cyclones form over warm oceans and can cause a lot of damage when they approach the shore. ☐

b A cyclone swept through the small town of Templeton early this morning, destroying buildings and uprooting trees. ☐

Student A: Ava's draft

The students in Ava's Year 6 class have to turn a story they have seen on television into a **newspaper report**.

Ava has chosen a story she saw recently about a British backpacker who got lost in the Tasmanian wilderness. This is how she organised her information.

Headline	THEY HAVE FOUND RICHARD MORGAN AFTER TEN DAYS
Who?	Richard Morgan, British backpacker
What?	Lost ten days
Where?	Tasmanian wilderness—Meander Falls, Alum Cliffs area
When?	Between 6 and 18 August
What happened next?	Found by bushwalkers—taken to hospital in Launceston
More information about the person involved	20 years old—from Nottingham, UK—staying at backpackers' hostel in Launceston
What people said	Dr Daniel Sutton: carrying out precautionary tests George Lumley, regional manager Parks and Wildlife Service: RM knew to stay warm and dry—has some bushcraft skills—had access to water Other tourists: saw RM at Meander Falls on 6 Aug—heading to Alum Cliffs area
Information for final paragraph	Parents in Nottingham—given up hope—going to fly to Australia—got text message—son alive

Proper nouns are the names of specific people, places and things. Some proper nouns consist of more than one word; for example, Meander Falls. All of the words in a proper noun start with a **capital letter**, except for some little words like *and* or *the.*
Look at Ava's notes and write down the name(s) of:

1. a city in the UK. ______
2. the British backpacker. ______
3. two places in Tasmania. ______
4. the person from the hospital. ______
5. the name of the organisation George Lumley works for. ______

Writing the first draft

Read Ava's **first draft** and then answer the questions.

They have found Richard Morgan after ten days

Richard Morgan was last seen ten days ago. Yesterday two bushwalkers found him.

Dr Daniel Sutton is one of the doctors treating Mr Morgan in Launceston General Hospital. He says Mr Morgan will remain in hospital until at least Sunday. They need to carry out some precautionary tests.

Mr Morgan has not talked to the media, so we don't know how he managed to survive in the wilderness for so long.

George Lumley works for the Parks and Wildlife Service. He says Mr Morgan must have some bushcraft skills. He knew to stay warm and dry. He also had access to water.

Mr Morgan is 20. He comes from Nottingham in the UK. He was last seen on 6 August. That was the day he went missing from his backpackers' hostel. Some tourists saw him at Meander Falls. He told them he was heading to the Alum Cliffs area.

Mr Morgan's parents had given up all hope for their son. They were just about to leave for Australia. Then they got a text message. It said he was alive and well.

1 A good **newspaper report** should contain the following features. Tick (✓) the ones that Ava has used.

- **a** a short **headline** that captures the reader's attention ☐
- **b** an **orientation** that tells **who**, **what**, **when**, and **where** ☐
- **c** a **retelling** of the events ☐
- **d** **quotes** or **statements** from witnesses or people involved ☐
- **e** interesting **information** and **detail** about people and events ☐
- **f** sentences that have the **correct spelling** and **punctuation** ☐
- **g** a **final paragraph** that wraps up the report ☐

2 The **tense** of the verbs often changes in newspaper reports. When writing about events that have already happened, reporters use the past tense; for example, *Some tourists* ***saw*** *him at Meander Falls.* When writing about events that are happening now, they use the present tense; for example, *He* ***says*** *Mr Morgan will remain in hospital.*

- **a** Underline three **present-tense verbs** in the second paragraph.
- **b** Underline the two **past-tense verbs** in the fourth paragraph (the one that starts *George Lumley …*)

Step-by-step improvement plan

Ava has done most things correctly in her draft **newspaper report**, but she could make some improvements. To find ways to do this, she is going to do some practice exercises. Help her complete them.

Step 1: Create a good headline

The **headline** is the heading at the top of a newspaper report or article. It should give the reader a clue about what the report or article is about.

To **capture** the reader's **attention**, and to encourage them to read the report, the headline should be interesting.

1. Ava has written three more **headlines** for her report. Which one is most likely to capture the reader's attention?

   a **RICHARD MORGAN WENT FOR A VERY LONG WALK** ☐

   b **BRITISH PACKPACKER ALIVE!** ☐

   c **BRITISH PACKPACKER'S ADVENTURE IN THE BUSH** ☐

2. Now write another good **headline** for Ava's report.

   ____

Step 2: Write a good introduction

The **introduction** is the opening paragraph or two of the report. It should set the scene by telling the reader **who** was involved, **what** happened, and **where**, **when** and sometimes **why** the events occurred.

Ava has left out some important information in her opening paragraphs. She also needs to tighten them up a bit.

Use the information in Ava's notes to complete these two separate **paragraphs**.

1. Richard Morgan, a (*what was he?*) ______________, who was last seen (*where?*) ______________ (*when?*) ______________, has been found by (*who?*) ______________

2. Mr Morgan, who is believed to have spent the last (*how long?*) ______________ in the bush, is now recovering (*where?*) ______________

Step 3: Include quotes

A **quote** repeats the **exact words** someone said. Including quotes from witnesses or people involved in the events **adds interest** to a newspaper report.

While Ava has included people's statements in her draft, they would have had more impact if she had written some of them as direct speech. For example:

Reported speech: Dr Daniel Sutton confirmed that Mr Morgan was receiving treatment and would remain in hospital until at least Sunday.

Direct speech: Dr Daniel Sutton confirmed that Mr Morgan was receiving treatment. "He will remain in hospital until at least Sunday," he said.

Hint! Make sure you put **speech marks** (" ") around the exact words someone says, including any punctuation. You might also have to change the **pronouns** and **tense** when writing reported speech as direct speech.

Rewrite each of the following statements so that the part in italics is in **direct speech**. Use the example above to help you.

1. Doctor Daniel Sutton says Mr Morgan will remain in hospital until at least Sunday *because they need to carry out some precautionary tests.*

   ____

   ____

2. George Lumley, regional manager of the Parks and Wildlife Service, said Mr Morgan obviously had some bush craft skills *because he knew to stay warm and dry.*

   ____

   ____

Step 4: Pack information into sentences

A **sentence** is a group of words that makes complete sense; for example, *He was found by two bushwalkers.* In newspaper reports, packing information from two or three sentences into one sentence makes your writing **tighter** and **easier to read**.

Ava could rewrite some of her sentences so that they contain more detail and read more fluently.

1. Use the prompts to help you turn the following paragraph into a **single sentence**.

   Mr Morgan is 20. He comes from Nottingham in the UK. He was last seen on 6 August. That was the day he went missing from his backpackers' hostel. Some tourists saw him at Meander Falls. He told them he was heading to the Alum Cliffs area.

   Mr Morgan, (*write the number that indicates his age*) __________, of (*write the name of the place he comes from in the UK*) ______________________, went missing from (*where?*) ______________________ on (*write down the date*) ______________

2. Now rewrite this paragraph as a **single sentence**.

   Mr Morgan's parents had given up all hope for their son. They were just about to leave for Australia. Then they got a text message. It said he was alive and well.

   ____

   ____

   ____

   ____

Writing the final draft

This is Ava's **final draft**. Read the comments about her **newspaper report** on the left, and do the tasks on the right.

Comments

A good **headline** *captures the reader's attention and tells* **what** *the report is about.*

A clear **orientation** *tells* **who**, **what**, **when** *and* **where**.

Including **quotes** *from witnesses or people involved brings the report alive.*

Adding **detail** *to sentences makes the report more interesting to read.*

The **conclusion** *wraps up the report.*

BRITISH BACKPACKER ALIVE!

Richard Morgan, the British backpacker who was last seen in the Meander Falls area ten days ago, has been found by two bushwalkers.

Mr Morgan, who has spent the last ten days in the bush, is now recovering in Launceston General Hospital.

Dr Daniel Sutton confirmed that Mr Morgan was in a stable condition, but said he would be kept under observation until at least Sunday. "We need to carry out some precautionary tests before we release him," he said.

Since he was found at 10 am on Thursday, Mr Morgan has not spoken about how he managed to keep himself alive during the freezing nights he spent alone in rugged and unfamiliar terrain.

George Lumley, regional manager of the Parks and Wildlife Service, answered reporters' questions about Mr Morgan's amazing survival story outside the hospital. "He obviously has some bushcraft skills and knew to stay warm and dry. There are lots of streams in the area, so he would have had access to water," he said.

Mr Morgan, 20, of Nottingham in the UK, went missing from his backpackers' hostel on 6 August. He was seen at the Meander Falls later that day, when he told a group of tourists he was heading to the Alum Cliffs area.

His parents in Nottingham had given up all hope for their son when the search entered its second week. They were due to fly to Australia when they received a text message informing them that Mr Morgan had been found alive and well.

Tasks

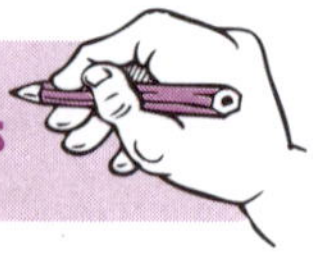

1. **Circle** the two **proper nouns**.
2. **Highlight** the **verb** that shows that **something happened before now**.
3. **Underline** the **quoted speech**.
4. **Circle** the **adjectives** that describe the terrain.
5. **Highlight** two **present-tense** verbs.
6. **Underline** the **information** Mr Morgan gave the tourists.
7. **Circle** the **proper nouns** that name places.

Student B: Jayden's draft

Jayden has relatives in Adelaide and has been following the news stories about bushfires in the region. He is going to write a **report** based on one of the stories.

While watching the news, he wrote down the following information. He also found these photos to go with his report.

Home destroyed after bushfire

Extinguishing fires from the air

Headline	**FIRES NEAR ADELAIDE**
Who?	Mike Bailey, farmer
What?	Bushfire on his property
Where?	70 km south of Adelaide
When?	10 am yesterday
What people said	Mike Bailey—flames 50 m from house—feared for his cattle—moved some—lost a paddock Country Fire Service spokesperson—60 firefighters—2 water-bombing helicopters—fire still out of control Lorenzo Russo (Bureau of Meteorology)—hot dry conditions—perfect for bushfires—cooler weather coming
Information for final paragraph	Rain expected—relief for fire fighters

Jayden can only use one of the photographs in his **report**. Which one do you think he should choose? Give a reason for your answer.

Writing the first draft

Read Jayden's **first draft** and then answer the questions.

> **A FIRE BREAKS OUT ON A PROPERTY SOUTH OF ADELAIDE**
>
> A large bushfire has broken out on farmer Mike Bailey's property.
>
> Mr Bailey said the flames came to within 50 m of his house. He feared for his cattle. He managed to move some of them, but he lost one of his paddocks.
>
> A Country Fire Service spokesperson said sixty firefighters and two water-bombing helicopters were trying to bring the blaze under control. So far they have been unsuccessful.
>
> Lorenzo Russo, who works for the Bureau of Meteorology, said the hot, dry conditions were making it difficult for the firefighters to contain the blaze. But luckily the weather will be cooler tomorrow.
>
> The Bureau of Meteorology is expecting rain to fall over the area. This will make it easier for the firefighters to bring the blaze under control.

1. A good **newspaper report** should contain the following features. Tick (✓) the ones that Jayden has included.

   a a short **headline** that captures the reader's attention ☐

   b an **orientation** that tells **who**, **what**, **when**, and **where** ☐

   c a **retelling** of the **events** ☐

   d **quotes** or **statements** from witnesses or people involved ☐

   e interesting **information** and **detail** about people and events ☐

   f sentences that have the **correct spelling** and **punctuation** ☐

   g a **final paragraph** that wraps up the report ☐

2. Jayden has used some good **vocabulary** in his draft.

   Which word or words has he used that mean the same as:

   a fire? ______________________

   b was worried about? ______________________

   c bring under control? ______________________

Step-by-step improvement plan

Jayden has written a good first draft, but there are things he could do to improve his **report**. Help him complete these practice exercises to find ways to do this.

Step 1: Create a good headline

Jayden's report needs a shorter, more attention-grabbing headline, so he has practised writing some different ones.

1. Tick the **headlines** that you think will make a bigger impact on readers, and also tell them what the report is about.

a FIRE DESTROYS PROPERTY, LIVESTOCK ☐

b COOLER WEATHER ON THE WAY ☐

c HEATWAVE SPARKS BUSHFIRE ☐

d HELP FROM THE SKIES ☐

2. Now use the following words to create a different **headline**.

CONTROL | OUT | BUSHFIRE | OF | RAGING

____

Step 2: Write a good introduction

Like Ava, Jayden has left out important information in his opening paragraphs. He also needs to tighten them up.

Fill in the missing **information** in the following sentences.

1. A large bushfire (*Where?*) ______________________________

(*What has it done?*) ______________________________

____

2. The fire started (*When?*) ______________________________

(*Where?*) ______________________________

______________________. Farmer Mike Bailey said he feared for

(*What did he fear for?*) ______________________ after flames came (*Where?*)

____

Step 3: Include quotes

Jayden can make his report more interesting by quoting the actual words some of the people involved said.

Rewrite the following sentences in **direct speech**, remembering that you might have to change the **pronouns** and **tenses**.

Hint! Re-read the rules for writing direct speech on page 5.

1. Mike Bailey said he had managed to move some of the cattle, but they had lost one of the paddocks.

____

____

____

2. Lorenzo Russo said the hot, dry conditions were making it difficult for the firefighters to contain the blaze.

____

____

____

Step 4: Pack information into sentences

1. Use the information in the following paragraph to complete the sentence below.

   A country fire service spokesperson said sixty firefighters were fighting the blaze. So were two water-bombing helicopters. They were trying to bring the blaze under control.

   A Country Fire Service spokesperson said sixty firefighters and ______________________________

   ______________________________ have so far been unable

   ____

2. Now turn each paragraph below into a **single sentence**.

   a Lorenzo Russo works for the Bureau of Meteorology. He said the situation should start to ease tomorrow. A cool change is going to blow in.

   ____

   ____

   ____

   b Much-needed rain is expected to fall over the area. The rain will bring relief. The firefighters will welcome it.

   ____

   ____

   ____

Writing the final draft

Jayden has started writing the **final draft** of his **report**. Help him complete it by filling in the missing sections, and then look in the answers section to compare what you have written with what Jayden wrote.

Hint! Look at Jayden's draft and the practice exercises for ideas.

FIRE DESTROYS PROPERTY, LIVESTOCK

A large bushfire south of Adelaide has destroyed sheds, crops and livestock.

The fire started … **(Use the practice exercises to help you write the next three paragraphs.)**

Much-needed rain is expected to fall over the area, bringing welcome relief to weary firefighters.

Your turn

Write a **newspaper report** of one to two pages on one of the following. Use your own paper for this activity.

Writing Checklist Make sure your recount includes: ✓

- a short **headline** that captures the reader's attention. ☐
- an **orientation** that tells **who**, **what**, **when**, and **where**. ☐
- a **retelling** of the events. ☐
- **quotes** or **statements** from witnesses or people involved. ☐
- interesting **information** and **detail** about people and events. ☐
- sentences that have the **correct spelling** and **punctuation**. ☐
- a **final paragraph** that wraps up the report. ☐

Tip Use **Ava's final draft** on page 6 and **Jayden's final draft** on page 11 to help you write your report.

Go to WORD BANK page 121 for useful vocabulary

1. Turn a news story that you have seen on television into a newspaper report.
2. Write a report for the newsletter about something that happened at school. You could write about an excursion you went on, a special event that was held at the school or anything else that you found interesting. Remember to write it like a newspaper report.
3. Write a newspaper report based on one of these photographs:

Unit 2 Restaurant reviews

Looking at reviews

A **review** is a text in which you give your personal **opinions** about something. You can review books, plays, films or places such as restaurants.

In this unit we will be reviewing a restaurant.

A **restaurant review** should have:

- an **introduction** that names the restaurant and tells where it is.
- middle **paragraphs** that give more detail and opinions about the food, service, etc.
- a **conclusion** that contains your overall opinion of the restaurant.

Read the following **review** and then answer the questions.

On Saturday morning my mum and I went to the new coffee shop in our local shopping centre. It's called Café au Lait and it's next to the bookshop.

It's decorated in dark colours, with soft lighting, which makes it feel cosy. There are also comfortable leather chairs for customers to sit on.

A waiter came quickly to take our order, but we had to wait quite a while for our drinks and food to arrive.

I had a strawberry milkshake and a choc-chip muffin. The milkshake was delicious, but my choc-chip muffin was a bit dry. Mum had a cappuccino and some banana bread. She said they were both perfect.

I think Café au Lait is average. The service wasn't good, but that could be because the shop is still quite new. I'll go there again once they've had time to sort out their problems.

1 What information has the writer included in the **introduction**? Tick (✓) the correct answers.

- **a** the name of the coffee shop ☐
- **b** why she went there ☐
- **c** where you can find the coffee shop ☐
- **d** when she went there ☐

2 Which **adjective** describes:

- **a** the feel of the coffee shop? ____________________
- **b** the leather chairs? ____________________
- **c** the milkshake? ____________________
- **d** the choc-chip muffin? ____________________

Student A: Anton's draft

The owners of Molto Delizioso, the new Italian restaurant near Anton's school, invited a group of students to try their menu and give suggestions on how they could improve the restaurant. Anton is going to write a **review** of the restaurant for the school newsletter.

These were some of the items on the menu:

a

b

c

1 Fill in the following **descriptions** under the correct photograph.

cool and refreshing	crunchy and chewy	sweet and creamy

2 Which of the following is the healthiest choice?

- **a** *coffee with milk and sugar* ☐
- **b** *a soft drink* ☐
- **c** *fresh orange juice* ☐

3 Use the photos above to help you complete the following sentence.

On the menu were ______________________________

Writing the first draft

This is the **first draft** of Anton's review. Read what he has written and then answer the questions.

> I went with some Year 6 students to the new restaurant near our school.
>
> I ordered the chicken and raspberry pizza. I like eating unusual food. It was good. I can recommend it. The crust was just the way I like it.
>
> There were lots of desserts to choose from. I had a banana split pizza. The waiter put chocolate chips on the ice cream and caramel sauce over everything. I really liked it.
>
> To drink, I had watermelon juice. The straw was shaped like a musical note!
>
> After our meal we had to fill in a questionnaire. I gave them top marks for their food and service. I said I didn't like the music.
>
> I really liked the food at the restaurant. I will tell my parents about it. I would like to go there again.

1 A good **restaurant review** should contain the following features. Tick (✓) the ones that Anton has used in his draft.

- **a** an **introduction** that **names** the restaurant and tells **where** it is ☐
- **b** middle **paragraphs** that contain more **detail** and **opinions** about the food, service, etc. ☐
- **c** interesting **adjectives** (e.g. *delicious food, outstanding service*) ☐
- **d** **correct spelling** and **punctuation** ☐
- **e** a **conclusion** that contains his **overall opinion** of the restaurant ☐

2 The dish that is served after the main course is called a dessert. What do we call:

a the dish that is served before the main course?

a casserole ☐	an entrée ☐	a sorbet ☐

b a small amount of food eaten between meals?

a starter ☐	a sweet ☐	a snack ☐

c food that is not part of a set menu, but can be ordered as separate items?

à la carte ☐	à la mode ☐	à la king ☐

d the salt, herbs or spices that are added to food for flavour?

grating ☐	seasoning ☐	mincing ☐

Step-by-step improvement plan

Anton wants to improve his **review**, so he is going to do some practice exercises to find ways to do this. Help him complete them.

Step 1: Start with a good introduction

The **introduction** is the opening paragraph. It should contain the **name** of the restaurant and some interesting **background information**, such as **when** and **why** you went there.

Starting with a good introduction gets your readers' attention and makes them want to read further.

Below are two different ways Anton could start his **introduction**. Complete them, making sure you include all of the key information.

1 On Wednesday I went with a group of Year 6s ______________________________

____

____

2 The owners of Molto Delizioso, the new ______________________________

____

____

Step 2: Use interesting adjectives

Adjectives give **information** about nouns and pronouns (e.g. *chilled juice*).

Using interesting adjectives **adds colour** to your writing.

Anton can make his review more interesting by using better adjectives to describe the food and express opinions.

Here are some adjectives Anton could use.

freshly squeezed	delicious	weird	old-fashioned	heavenly
crisp	refreshing	ice-cold	thin	outstanding

1 Complete the following sentences with **adjectives** from the box.

a Chicken and raspberries on a pizza might sound ________________, but it tasted ________________.

b My ________________________ watermelon juice was ________________ and very ________________.

2 Now use the remaining five **adjectives** to complete the answers to the following questions.

a What was the pizza crust like? The pizza crust ______________________________

____

b What did the banana split pizza taste like? The banana split pizza ________________

____

c What did you think of the music? I thought ______________________________

____

d What did you think of the service? I thought ______________________________

____

Step 3: Add interest with descriptive verbs

A **verb** shows that an **action** is happening, has happened or will happen. Some verbs are more descriptive than others.

For example: *She* ***dabbed*** *her mouth with her napkin.*

Dabbed is more descriptive than, for example, *cleaned,* because *dabbed* tells us exactly how she cleaned her mouth.

Using descriptive verbs helps your readers **visualise** the actions, and makes your writing more interesting to read.

Complete each sentence below with a descriptive **verb** from the box. Use each verb once.

drizzled	garnished	coated	ladled	sprinkled

1. The waiter ________________ the sauce over the steak.
2. The pasta was ________________ in a creamy sauce.
3. The waiter ________________ some chocolate chips over the ice-cream.
4. He ________________ caramel sauce over everything.
5. They ________________ the shrimp salad with sprigs of parsley.

Step 4: End with a good conclusion

The **conclusion** is the final paragraph. It should wrap up the review with the writer's **overall opinion** of the restaurant. It should also be interesting.

Anton has jotted down some ideas for his **conclusion**. Help him organise them into a **paragraph**.

Hint! You can check your answer by looking at Anton's final draft, but try to work it out yourself first.

will definitely tell parents about Molto Delizioso

excellent menu

healthy choices

their food—very delicious!

Molto Delizioso—'very delicious' in Italian (waiter told us)

____

____

____

____

Writing the final draft

This is Anton's **final draft**. Read the comments about his **review** on the left, and do the activities on the right.

Comments

A good ***introduction*** *gives the* ***name*** *of the restaurant and tells* ***where*** *it is.*

Using ***paragraphs*** *helps the writer organise his or her information.*

Using interesting ***adjectives*** *helps the writer express* ***opinions*** *about the restaurant.*

Using ***descriptive verbs*** *helps the reader* ***visualise*** *the actions.*

Giving your ***overall opinion*** *of the restaurant in an interesting way helps to wrap up the review.*

Restaurant review

On Wednesday I went with a group of Year 6s to Molto Delizioso, the new Italian restaurant near our school. The owners wanted our opinion on the menu, as well as any suggestions on how they could improve the restaurant.

I ordered the chicken and raspberry pizza because I like to try something different when I go to a restaurant. Chicken and raspberries on a pizza might sound weird, but it was delicious and I can definitely recommend it. The crust was thin and crisp, and the tomato sauce base and mozzarella cheese topping perfect.

They have a wide variety of desserts to choose from, such as gelato in every flavour, panna cotta and cassata, but I went for the banana split pizza. When the waiter brought it to the table, he sprinkled some chocolate chips over the ice-cream and drizzled caramel sauce over everything. It was heavenly!

Although you can order soft drinks and milkshakes, I had the freshly squeezed watermelon juice. It was ice-cold and very refreshing. They also have fresh orange, apple and pineapple juice. The straw in my drink was shaped like a musical note, which made it interesting to drink through.

At the end of our meal we were each given a questionnaire to fill in. I gave them top marks for their food and service, but I thought the music they played was a bit old-fashioned.

I will definitely be telling my parents about Molto Delizioso. They have an excellent menu with some healthy choices. Our waiter told us that Molto Delizioso means 'very delicious' in Italian, and that is exactly what their food is—very delicious!

Tasks

1. **Underline** the **words** that add information about Molto Delizioso.
2. **Highlight** the **adjective** that expresses Anton's opinion of the chicken and raspberry pizza.
3. **Circle** two **descriptive verbs**.
4. **Underline** the **list** of items.
5. **Highlight** the word that expresses Anton's **opinion** of the music.
6. **Underline** Anton's **overall opinion** of the food at the restaurant.

Student B: Divina's draft

Divina, another Year 6 student, was also part of the group that was invited to sample Molto Delizioso's menu. Her **review** of the restaurant is also going to appear in the school's newsletter.

At the restaurant, Divina took a photo of her dessert. She also jotted down some of the items on the menu in her notebook.

Spicy Chicken Cacciatore
Mushroom Risotto
Almond Cheesecake
Braised Lamb Shanks
Zucchini Fries
Beef Braciole
Raspberry Panna Cotta
Baked Eggplant
Double Chocolate Biscotti
Italian Sausage, Peppers and Onions

1. Help Divina organise the menu items under the following headings:

Meat and Poultry

___

___

___

___

Vegetarian

___

___

___

Dessert

___

___

___

2. If you had to choose three items from the above menu, which would they be?

Start your answer like this: If I had to ___

___

___

___

Writing the first draft

This is Divina's **first draft**. Read it and then answer the questions.

On Wednesday some Year 6 students went to Molto Delizioso, the new Italian restaurant near our school, to try out their menu. I was lucky enough to go with them.

The colours in the restaurant are green, white and red. Those are the colours of the Italian flag. The walls are red and white. The tablecloths are green and white. There are pictures of Italy on the walls. I liked the colours. They made me feel good.

I had the Pasta Napolitana. They used fresh tomatoes to make the sauce. I could tell. I cook a lot with Mum at home. It was really nice.

For dessert I had Cannoli with Vanilla Custard. It had cream and icing sugar on the top. I really liked it. My apple juice was also good. It was fresh apple juice.

I've been to lots of Italian restaurants. This one has the best menu. There were lots of yummy things on the menu. There were things like taco pizza and dessert pizzas.

We filled in a questionnaire at the end. I gave Molto Delizioso five stars. The service was good. The waiters were friendly. The food was good.

1. Which of these features has Divina remembered to include in her draft? Tick (✓) the ones that she has used.
   - **a** an **introduction** that **names** the restaurant and tells **where** it is ☐
   - **b** middle **paragraphs** that contain more **detail** and **opinions** about the food, service, etc. ☐
   - **c** interesting **adjectives** ☐
   - **d** **correct spelling** and **punctuation** ☐
   - **e** a **conclusion** that contains her **overall opinion** of the restaurant ☐

2. In the first paragraph, which word could Divina use in place of *try out*?

   a attempt ☐ **b** sample ☐ **c** inspect ☐

3. Which word could Divina use to correctly complete the following sentence?

   The restaurant is ____________________ in the colours of the Italian flag.

4. In Divina's draft, which of the following words could best be used in place of *questionnaire*?

   a test ☐ **b** interview ☐ **c** survey ☐

Step-by-step improvement plan

Divina is also going to do some practice exercises to find ways to improve her draft. Help her complete them.

Step 1: Write better sentences

A **sentence** is a group of words that makes complete sense. It consists of one or more **clauses**.

A **simple sentence** contains **one main clause**. That means it has **one subject** and **one verb**.

For example: *The restaurant* (**subject**) *is* (**verb**) *near our school.*

It is often better to combine simple sentences into longer **compound** or **complex sentences**.

A **compound sentence** contains **two or more main clauses**. The clauses are joined with the **conjunctions** *and, but, or* and *so.*

For example: *The walls are red and white. The tablecloths are green and white.*
The walls are red and white **and** *the tablecloths are green and white.*

A **complex sentence** contains a **main** and a **subordinate clause**, or a clause that depends on the main clause for its meaning. The clauses in a complex sentence can be joined with

- a **conjunction** such as *because, if, when, while, unless* or *until.*
- a **relative pronoun** such as *who, whose, that* or *which.*

For example: *For dessert I had Cannoli with Vanilla Custard. I really liked it.*
For dessert I had Cannoli with Vanilla Custard, **which** *I really liked.*

Using a variety of sentence types makes your writing more interesting to read.

Join the following simple sentences to make longer **compound** or **complex sentences**.

1. The restaurant is decorated in green, white and red. These are the colours of the Italian flag. ______________________________
____
____

2. The sauce had been made with fresh tomatoes. I knew. I cook a lot with Mum at home. We often make Napolitana sauce. ______________________________
____
____

3. My apple juice was also good. It had been freshly squeezed. ______________________________
____
____

4. I've been to lots of Italian restaurants. This one definitely has the best choice of food.
____
____

Step 2: Use interesting adjectives

Divina's review would be more interesting to read if she used better adjectives to express her opinions about the restaurant and the food.

1. Help her choose **adjectives** from the box to replace the ones that have been underlined. Use each adjective once.

tasty	bright	mouth-watering	divine	amazing	happy

a The nice ________________ colours made me feel good ________________ straight away.

b The Pasta Napolitana was very nice ________________________.

c There is only one word to describe the dessert—great ________________________!

d My freshly squeezed apple juice was also good ________________________.

e There are also yummy ________________________ desserts on the menu.

2. If Divina had *not* liked the food at the restaurant, she could have used the following **adjectives** to express her opinions about it.

tasteless | boring | dry | tough | unappealing

Choose at least two of the adjectives to write more negative opinions of the Pasta Napolitana and the dessert.

a ____

____

b ____

____

Step 3: Add detail and interest with noun phrases

Noun phrases are groups of words that are built around nouns. They can include **articles** (*a, an, the*), **pronouns** (e.g. *his, my*), **adjectives** (e.g. *delicious, horrible*) and other phrases (e.g. *of salt*). They are a way of **adding detail** and **interest** to sentences.

dusting	scattering	swirl	splash	ripple

Complete each of the following sentences with a word from the box, and then underline the longest **noun phrase** in each sentence.

1. The dessert was topped off with a ________________________ of cream.
2. A ________________________ of raspberry ran through the vanilla ice-cream.
3. The chef added a ________________________ of oil to the pan.
4. There was a ________________________ of finely chopped herbs around the plate.
5. The cannoli were covered in a light ________________________ of icing sugar.

Writing the final draft

Divina has started writing the **final draft** of her **review**. Help her complete it, and then look in the answers section to compare what you have written with what Divina wrote.

Hint! Look at Divina's draft and the practice exercises to complete this exercise.

Restaurant review

On Wednesday some Year 6 students were invited to sample the menu at Molto Delizioso, the new Italian restaurant near our school. I was lucky enough to be one of them.

(Write about the way the restaurant is decorated and how it made Divina feel.)

....

....

....

....

....

....

I started with the Pasta Napolitana. I could tell that the pasta sauce had been made with fresh tomatoes because I cook a lot with Mum at home and we often make Napolitana sauce. The pasta was perfect—not too hard and not too mushy. Our waiter told us the word for that is *al dente*.

(Write about Divina's dessert and drink and her opinions of them.)

....

....

....

....

....

....

(Write about Divina's opinion of the choice of food at the restaurant and some of the items on offer on the menu.)

....

....

....

....

....

....

When it came to filling in the questionnaire at the end of the meal, I gave Molto Delizioso five stars for their friendly waiters, excellent service and delicious food.

Your turn

Write a **review** of one of the following. Use your own paper for this activity.

Writing Checklist Make sure your review includes: ✓

- an **introduction** that **names** the restaurant and tells **where** it is. ☐
- a **middle section** that contains more **detail** and **opinions** about the food, service, etc. ☐
- interesting **adjectives**. ☐
- **correct spelling** and **punctuation**. ☐
- a **conclusion** that contains your **overall opinion** of the restaurant. ☐

Tip Use **Anton's final draft** on page 18 and **Divina's final draft** on page 23 to help you write your review.

Go to WORD BANK page 121 for useful vocabulary

1. Write a review of your favourite restaurant.
2. Write a review of a restaurant where you were not impressed with either the food or the service, or both.
3. Imagine you have recently eaten at a restaurant called The Bug Inn, where these were the only items on the menu. Write a review of your experience.

STARTERS

Dried caterpillars garnished with a sprinkling of fresh herbs

Crunchy cockroaches coated in a mixture of aromatic spices

MAINS

Deep-fried spiders drenched in caramel

Awesome frogs' legs served with a lemon and butter sauce

DESSERTS

Banana worm bread

Chocolate-covered grasshoppers

Unit 3 Descriptions—photographs

Looking at descriptions

A **description** can be **imaginative** or **informative**, depending on its context. Its aim is to give the reader a clearer picture of a person, place or thing, often by using **figurative language**.

A description is usually part of another text. In a **narrative**, for example, its **purpose** is to **help tell the story**; in an **advertisement**, it **helps sell** the product; and in a **report** or **explanation**, its main purpose is to **inform**.

However, a description can be a text on its own. In this case, it should have:

- an interesting **introduction** that captures the reader's attention and briefly tells **what** the description is about.
- a **series** of **paragraphs** that **describe** the subject.
- a **conclusion** that contains a **final comment** or **thought** about the person, place or thing.

You can find **descriptions** in most types of text:

recounts | narratives | poems | diary entries | newspaper and magazine articles | advertisements | information reports | letters and emails

1 In which type of text are you most likely to find the following **descriptions**?

a She looked up at the sky. Grey clouds were bunched together, like piles of dirty laundry.

____

b They have powerful hind legs and short, thumbless forelimbs, while their bodies are covered in thick, coarse, woolly hair.

____

c An elephant has a very long trunk
Its coat is rough and grey
Its legs are thick and mighty strong
This beast is no one's prey.

____

2 Which of the following **descriptions** is more likely to be part of an advertisement?

a This sleek, reliable little car comes in a variety of colours. ☐

b Our neighbours' new car is metallic blue, with tinted windows and a sun roof. ☐

Student A: Lilian's draft

Lilian's Year 6 class has been learning about descriptions. The students have to choose a **photograph** that they particularly like and **describe** its **contents** and any **feelings** they might experience when looking at it. They are going to call their descriptions *A moment in time.*

Lilian has chosen the following photograph, which she took herself. She started by pasting a copy of the photograph into her notebook, and then she wrote down some words around it.

1 Which of the following objects in the photograph could be **described** as:

a tall and thin? ____________________

b short and round? ____________________

c long and straight? ____________________

d ridged and rugged? ____________________

e dark and ghostly? ____________________

2 When we look at an image on a flat surface, like a painting or photograph, objects in the distance seem smaller and further away than they are, relative to their size. This is known as **perspective**.

a Which object in the photograph would actually be the tallest? ____________________

b Which objects appear taller because of perspective? ____________________

____

Writing the first draft

This is Lilian's **first draft**. Read what she has written and then answer the questions.

A moment in time

I took this photograph one morning. Everything before me was beautiful. Everything was in harmony.

Before me was a straight road. There were rugged mountains in the background. There were hedges next to the road. They had been neatly clipped. Behind the hedges were some fir and olive trees. The fir trees were tall and thin and the olive trees were shorter and puffy.

The trees made shadows on the road. The fir trees' shadows reached right across the road and over the hedge on the other side. The olive trees' shadows only came halfway across the road. The tops of the fir trees were a bit ruffled.

The mountains at the back went up and down in an uneven way. They looked magnificent.

As I walked down the road, I tried not to step on the shadows. I didn't want to disturb this magical scene.

1 A good **description** should contain the following features. Tick (✓) the ones that Lilian has used in her draft.

- **a** an interesting **introduction** that captures the reader's attention and briefly tells **what** the description is about ☐
- **b** a **series** of **paragraphs** that describe the subject ☐
- **c** interesting **adjectives** (e.g. *rugged, ruffled*) ☐
- **d** descriptive **verbs** (e.g. *dipped, gleamed*) ☐
- **e** **similes** and **metaphors** (e.g. *The fir trees were tall and ended in points, like pencils. The sky was a clear blue canopy over our heads.*) ☐
- **f** **correct spelling** and **punctuation** ☐
- **g** a **conclusion** that contains a **final comment** or **thought** about the person, place or thing ☐

2 Which **adjectives** has Lilian used to describe:

- **a** the appearance of the olive trees? ______________________
- **b** the appearance of the mountain top? ______________________
- **c** her opinion of the mountains? ______________________
- **d** the scene she was looking at? ______________________

3 Combine the three sentences in the introduction to form a **single sentence**. Start like this:

On the morning I took ____

____

____

Step-by-step improvement plan

Lilian has written a satisfactory first draft, but she wants to make her **description** more interesting. She is going to do some practice exercises to find ways to do this and needs your help to complete them.

Step 1: Add interest with similes and metaphors

A **simile** is a **figure of speech** that uses the words *like* or *as* to compare two things that are unlike each other.

For example: *The mountain peak was* **like** *a tall tower. The road was* **as** *smooth* **as** *glass.*

Using **similes** to describe people, places and things makes your writing **more interesting** to read.

1 To which object can the following most effectively be **compared**? Circle your choice.

a	the shadows of the olive trees	circles	pools	moons
b	the shadows of the fir trees	long fingers	ruled lines	crooked sticks
c	the paving on the road	boxes	a graph	a checkerboard
d	the hedges	armchairs	benches	stools
e	the grey colour of the road	a forest	the sea	slate

A **metaphor** is a **figure of speech** that makes a direct comparison between two unlike things, without using the words *like* or *as*.

For example: *The mountain peak was a tall tower in the distance.*

The road is the portal to our destination.

Like similes, metaphors **add interest** to a description.

2 Turn the following similes into **metaphors**. Rewrite the underlined parts only.

a The leaves on the olive trees were like shimmering sequins.

____

b The shadows were like ghosts blocking the travellers' way.

____

3 Now write an interesting sentence in which you use a **metaphor** to compare the line of trees to punctuation marks. ______________________________

____

Step 2: Bring objects to life with personification

Personification is a form of **metaphor** in which animals and objects are given human qualities.

For example: *The fir trees stood proudly to attention, like sentinels on guard.*

Using personification in descriptions **adds interest** by bringing objects to life.

1. Highlight the expression that **personifies** each object in the following sentences.
   a. The shadows of the fir trees lay like long, thin (pencils, fingers, threads) across the road.
   b. The trees (danced, bent, moved) in the light breeze.
   c. The tops of the trees (bobbed up and down, moved from side to side, nodded politely to each other).
2. Now write a good sentence in which you:
   a. give the sun human qualities, e.g. it could be looking at something.

      ____

      ____

   b. give the mountain human qualities, e.g. it could be wearing something.

      ____

      ____

Step 3: Add interest with descriptive verbs

In Unit 2 you learnt that a **verb** shows that an **action** is happening, has happened or will happen, and that some verbs are more **descriptive** and useful than others because they show exactly **how an action is performed**.

For example, in the sentences *The shadows* **moved** *across the road* and *The shadows* **crept** *across the road,* the second sentence is more descriptive because it gives us a better image of *how* the shadows moved.

Using **descriptive verbs** can therefore add a great deal of **interest** and **energy** to your writing.

Hint! Descriptive verbs are often used to **personify objects**, as in the example above.

Below are a number of **verbs**. Choose the most **descriptive** one to complete each of the following sentences.

moved	avoided	created	thrown	hooked	made	conjured	lay
etched	cast	was	were	fell	skirted	swayed	written

1. Before me ____________ a straight road.
2. Close-clipped hedges ____________ protective barriers on either side of the road.
3. The trees ____________ shadows on the smooth surface of the road.
4. The long shadows ____________ themselves over the hedge on the opposite side.
5. The fir trees ____________ gently in the light breeze.
6. Behind the trees the mountains were sharply ____________ against the clear blue sky.
7. I carefully ____________ the pools of shadow, not wishing to disturb the magical scene that nature had ____________ up.

Writing the final draft

This is Lilian's **final draft**. Read the comments about her **description** on the left, and do the tasks on the right.

Comments

Tasks

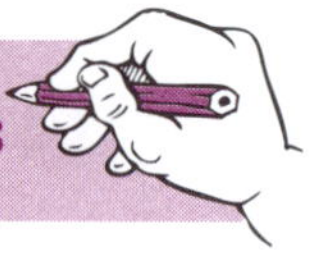

A moment in time

The **introduction** *briefly tells what the description is about.*

I took this photograph because I was struck by the harmony and beauty of my surroundings.

1. Circle two **abstract nouns**.

Inserting an **image** *of the object or scene being described helps to focus the reader's attention.*

Using **interesting adjectives** *adds interest to the description.*

Before me lay a straight road, with rugged mountains in the background. Close-clipped hedges created protective barriers on either side of the road, and a line of trees, arranged so that the smaller olive trees alternated with the taller fir trees, like a series of full stops and exclamation marks, rose behind each hedge. The olive trees made up for their lack of height by puffing themselves out, while the fir trees stood proudly to attention, like sentinels on guard.

2. Highlight two **similes**.

Using **similes** *and* **metaphors** *helps the reader visualise what is being described.*

The trees with the sun behind them cast shadows on the smooth surface of the road, as though trying to stamp their authority on it. Those cast by the fir trees reached across the road, hooking themselves over the hedge on the opposite side, like long, thin fingers.

3. Underline three words or phrases that help to **personify** the trees.

Using **personification** *brings inanimate objects to life.*

The tufty tops of the fir trees swayed gently in the light breeze as they nodded politely to each other. Behind them the mountains were sharply etched against the clear blue sky, their bumps and ridges like the back of a sleeping dragon.

4. Circle three **descriptive verbs**.

Concluding with a **comment** *or* **thought** *about the person, place or thing neatly wraps up the description.*

As I walked down the road, I carefully skirted the pools of shadow, not wishing to disturb the magical scene that Nature had conjured up.

5. Highlight the **metaphor**.

Student B: Ari's draft

Ari, another Year 6 student, is also going to describe a photograph he took himself.

Like Lilian, he started by pasting a copy of the photograph in his notebook and then made some brief notes around it.

felt excited

still water

two boats

sturdy building on solid rock

cables stretched tightly

smoke coming from island

mountain below

buildings below tiny

narrow roads

1 This photograph shows a lot of the landscape, so it is what is known as a long shot. It has also been taken from a high angle, with the camera looking down on the scene below.

If this were a scene from a movie, what effect might the director be hoping to achieve? Tick (✓) the most likely answer.

a To make the objects below look cute and appealing. ☐

b To make the objects below look scary and threatening. ☐

c To make the objects below look small and defenceless. ☐

2 In the phrase *cables stretched tightly*, which word could best replace *tightly*?

a compactly ☐ | **b** tautly ☐ | **c** securely ☐

3 What do you think is the purpose of the cables? ______________________________

____

Writing the first draft

This is Ari's **first draft**. Read what he wrote and then answer the questions.

A moment in time

Standing on top of that mountain and looking down at the scene below made me feel on top of the world—literally and figuratively.

Far below me I could see buildings and playing fields. They looked tiny. There were also lots of narrow roads. To my left were the cables along which the car travels up and down the mountain. They were stretched tightly and looked as if they could easily snap. They ended up in a sturdy building that stood on solid rock.

Below was another mountain. It was long and low, but ended in a higher point.

Beyond the mountain was the sea. It was very calm. There were two boats on the water, and to their right was an island. There must have been a fire on the island because smoke was coming from it.

I love this photograph. Whenever I need cheering up, all I have to do is look at this photo and I feel happy again.

1. Which of these features has Ari remembered to include in his draft? Tick (✓) the ones that he has used.

   a an interesting **introduction** that captures the reader's attention and briefly tells **what** the description is about ☐

   b a **series** of **paragraphs** that describe the subject ☐

   c interesting **adjectives** ☐

   d descriptive **verbs** ☐

   e **similes** and **metaphors** ☐

   f **correct spelling** and **punctuation** ☐

   g a **conclusion** that contains a **final comment** or **thought** about the person, place or thing ☐

2. What do you think Ari means when he says that standing on top of the mountain made him feel on top of the world—*literally and figuratively*?

   ____

   ____

   ____

   ____

3. Ari says that the cables looked as if they could easily snap. Which of the following adjectives could best replace *as if they could easily snap*? Tick (✓) the correct answer.

   slender ☐ faint ☐ fragile ☐ poor ☐ faulty ☐

Step-by-step improvement plan

Ari also wants to make his description more interesting, so he is going to do some practice exercises to find ways to do this. Help him complete them.

Step 1: Add interest with similes and metaphors

1 Which item can each of the following objects from Ari's photograph be **compared** to? Tick (✓) the best option.

a the pattern formed by the buildings and playing fields

an abstract painting ☐	a portrait ☐	a drawing ☐

b the roads on the mountain below

long sticks ☐	little pencils ☐	narrow ribbons ☐

c the fragile-looking cables along which the cars travel

a spider's web ☐	lengths of rope ☐	rubber bands ☐

d the building where the cables end

a hotel ☐	a skyscraper ☐	a fortress ☐

e the island out to sea

a turtle's shell ☐	a huge whale ☐	a yacht ☐

2 Complete each of the following sentences with a **simile**. Use the comparisons above to help you.

a Far below me lay buildings and playing fields, ______________________________

____

b The cables along which the car travels up and down the mountain were stretched tautly,

____

c The cables disappeared into a sturdy building that stood ______________________

____

3 Write your own sentences about the roads and the island, making sure they contain **similes**.

a ____

____

b ____

____

4. Look at Ari's photograph carefully before answering the following questions.
   a. What can the ocean most effectively be compared to? Tick (✓) the best answer.

      a glossy marble floor ☐   a slab of ice ☐   a sheet of tranquil blue ☐

   b. What can the smoke most effectively be compared to? Tick (✓) the best answer.

      a fine mist ☐   a steady drizzle ☐   a dark cloud ☐

   c. Now write an interesting sentence about the ocean, using the comparisons above to help you include a **metaphor**.

Tip! Look at the notes in the previous section to remind yourself of the difference between a simile and a metaphor.

____

____

Step 2: Bring objects to life with personification

An object in the photograph that could be **personified** is the rocky outcrop that juts out from the top of the mountain below. If you look at it carefully, you'll notice that it looks a bit like an ancient Egyptian pharaoh.

1. What might it be doing? Tick (✓) the best answer.

   a waving to the boats ☐   b scanning the horizon ☐   c striding towards the water ☐

2. What might it be wearing?   a a blazer ☐   b gloves ☐   c a cloak ☐

3. Write two interesting sentences that **personify** the rocky outcrop, one describing what it is doing and the other describing what it is wearing.

   a ____

   ____

   b ____

   ____

Step 3: Add interest with descriptive verbs

1. In the following sentences, circle the **verb** that most effectively completes the sentence.
   a. Buildings and playing fields (marked, smudged, speckled) the landscape.
   b. Narrow roads (threaded, bent, swivelled) their way across the open countryside.
   c. The cables were (looped, strung, fastened) tautly against the backdrop of the blue water.
   d. The island looked like a giant whale (blowing, puffing, spouting) a fine mist from its blowhole.
   e. Two boats (drifted, wandered, navigated) lazily on the still water.
   f. A rocky outcrop on the mountain below (looked, peeped, gazed) out to sea.

2. If the slopes of the mountain are compared to a cloak that a pharaoh is wearing, which three words best describe how it moves about him? Tick the correct answers.

   a swirls ☐   b billows ☐   c coils ☐   d curves ☐   e flows ☐

Writing the final draft

Ari has started writing the **final draft** of his **description**. Help him complete it and then look in the answers section to compare what you have written with what Ari wrote.

Hint! Look at Ari's draft and the practice exercises to complete this exercise.

A moment in time

On the day I took this photograph I was feeling on top of the world—literally because I was standing on top of a mountain looking down on the world, and figuratively because I was excited to be there. **(Write about the buildings, playing fields, roads and cables.)**

(Write about the ocean and the island.)

Two boats closer to shore drifted lazily on the still water, apparently unconcerned by the threat the creature might pose. **(Write about the rocky outcrop on the mountain below.)**

Now, whenever I feel downcast, all I have to do to recapture the sense of elation I experienced that day is look at this photograph.

Your turn

Write a **description** of about a page of one of the following. Use your own paper for this activity.

Writing Checklist Make sure your description includes: ✓

- an interesting **introduction** that captures the reader's attention and briefly tells **what** the description is about. ☐
- a **series** of **paragraphs** that describe the subject. ☐
- interesting **adjectives**. ☐
- descriptive **verbs**. ☐
- **similes**, **metaphors** and **personification**. ☐
- **correct spelling** and **punctuation**. ☐
- a **conclusion** that contains a **final comment** or **thought** about the person, place or thing. ☐

Tip Use **Lilian's final draft** on page 30 and **Ari's final draft** on page 35 to help you write your descriptions.

Go to WORD BANK page 121 for useful vocabulary

1. Describe a photograph that you particularly like.
2. Write a description of one of the photographs below.

Unit 4 Expositions—editorials

Looking at expositions

An **exposition** is a text that expresses a particular **position** or **point of view** and gives evidence to support it. Its main purpose is to **persuade** people that this particular point of view is the correct one.

We can persuade others to believe or do something during a normal conversation. However, we also make speeches and write letters, emails, editorials and blogs to try to persuade others to our point of view.

In this unit we will be looking at **editorials**.

Editorials are **newspaper** or **magazine articles** in which the editor expresses his or her **opinion** on an issue or topic that is discussed elsewhere in the publication or that is being debated in the community. These articles may appear in a paper publication or online.

An **editorial**, like most expositions, should have:

- an **introduction** that states the writer's main **opinion** or **point of view**.
- **arguments** that give **reasons** for the point of view.
- **evidence** to **support** the **arguments**.
- a **conclusion** that **repeats** the **main opinion** and **refers back** briefly to the **arguments**.

1. Which of the following sentences expresses an **opinion**?

   a Some animals in zoos are kept in cages. ☐

   b It is cruel to keep animals in cages. ☐

2. If someone recommended that you read a particular book, which statement below would be most likely to **persuade** you?

   a You might want to read this book. It's about a lion, an eagle and a snake. Each one thinks he is the strongest of all the animals. ☐

   b You must read this fantastic book. It's about a lion, an eagle and a snake. Each one thinks he is the strongest of all the animals. ☐

   c This is a book about a lion, an eagle and a snake. Each one thinks he is the strongest of all the animals. I enjoyed it. ☐

3. Look at your answer for Question 2. Explain why you think this is the most **persuasive** statement.

   ____

   ____

Student A: Angus's draft

Angus's Year 6 class have been discussing what it means to be a good citizen. They have put forward many ideas, but have finally decided that all their suggestions can be summed up in the following two sentences:

- A good citizen respects the rights of others.
- A good citizen respects the environment.

Each student now has to imagine that he or she is the editor of the school newspaper, writing the **editorial** that will appear on the front page. They can express their views on EITHER why it is important to respect the rights of others, OR why it is important to respect the environment. Their teacher will then select the best piece to go on the front page of the newspaper.

Angus is going to write about why it is important to respect the rights of others. He starts by **organising** his **thoughts** and **ideas**.

Arguments	Supporting evidence
Introduction: Amnesty International—all humans have right to "basic freedoms and protections". Not always the case. Need to learn to respect rights of others—safer world	
Argument 1: People who don't respect rights of others to be different can become bullies—cause problems for their victims and themselves	Problems for victims—can become anxious, lonely—schoolwork could suffer Problem for bullies—can get into serious trouble
Argument 2: People who don't respect rights of others can become criminals—ruin their lives and their victims' lives	Problems for victims—can become nervous, anxious—don't want to leave their homes Problem for criminals—can go to jail if caught
Argument 3: People don't respect other people's religion or way of life—can lead to wars	Wars cause suffering
Conclusion: If more people learn to respect others—world would be a safer place	

What are some of the ways innocent people suffer during wars? Fill in at least two pieces of supporting evidence in the box for Argument 3.

Writing the first draft

This is Angus's **first draft**. Read what he wrote and then answer the questions.

Why it is important to respect the rights of others

Amnesty International says all humans have the right to "basic freedoms and protections". That means all people have the right to feel safe. This doesn't always happen. We must learn to respect the rights of others. Then the world will be safer.

Some people don't respect the right of others to be different. They bully them. Bullying is a big problem in many schools. It's a problem in our school. Bullies don't respect others. Children who get bullied are scared to go to school. The bullies can get into serious trouble. Bullying is bad for the bullies and for their victims. People must start respecting each other. Then there won't be so much bullying.

Some people who don't respect the rights of others become criminals. Crime is a big problem in our society. Criminals have no respect for others. They steal from them. They make them scared. People might not want to leave their homes. The criminals can end up in jail. People must learn to respect others and their property. Then there won't be so much crime.

Some people don't respect the beliefs and way of life of others. This can lead to wars. War is a big problem in the world. Lots of innocent people suffer in wars. People must learn to respect other people's religion and culture. Then there won't be so many wars.

People must learn to respect others. Then the world will be a safer place.

1 A good **exposition** should contain the following features. Tick (✓) the ones that Angus has used.

- **a** an **introduction** that states the **main opinion** or **point of view** ☐
- **b** a series of **arguments** that give **reasons** for the point of view ☐
- **c** **evidence** to **support** the **arguments** ☐
- **d** **modal verbs** (e.g. *must, can*) ☐
- **e** **modal adverbs** (e.g. *definitely, maybe*) ☐
- **f** **present-tense** verbs (e.g. *respect, steal*) ☐
- **g** **connectives** to link arguments (e.g. *for example, finally*) ☐
- **h** a separate **paragraph** for each **argument** ☐
- **i** **correct spelling** and **punctuation** ☐
- **j** a **conclusion** that **repeats** the **main opinion** and **refers back** to the **arguments** ☐

2 Use the information in Angus's draft to help you complete the following sentences.

a People who respect those who are different from them in some way ______________________

____

b One of the main reasons for wars is that ______________________

____

____

Step-by-step improvement plan

Angus would like his teacher to choose his editorial to appear in the school newspaper, but first he needs to find ways to improve it. Help him complete these exercises that contain tips on how he can do that.

Step 1: Use connectives to link ideas

Connectives are words and phrases that **link ideas** in a text. Many of them are **adverbs** or **prepositional phrases** (phrases that start with a preposition).

For example: *Bullying can cause problems for the victims.* ***Furthermore****, it can cause problems for the bullies themselves.*
Bullying can cause problems for the victims. ***In addition****, it can cause problems for the bullies themselves.*

Using **connectives** to link ideas helps to make the text read **more fluently**.

1. Complete the paragraph below with the **connectives** from the box. Use each connective once.

too	for example	on the other hand	also	on the one hand

When people do not respect the rights of others, it can cause many problems. Bullying, ____________________, is a problem in many schools. It is ______________ a problem in our school. Crime, ___________, can affect people badly. ______________________________, the victims of crime can become extremely frightened; ______________________________, the criminals can end up spending time in jail.

2. Circle the **connective** in brackets that best links the ideas in the following sets of sentences.

   a Children who get picked on by bullies often become anxious and lonely. (Otherwise, Instead, However), the bullies also make life difficult for themselves. (Even so, So, Anyway) bullying is bad for the bullies and their victims.

   b Criminals (also, then, indeed) lack respect for others. Thieves, (at once, for instance, rather), take what isn't theirs. (Whenever, In the end, Moreover), they often threaten innocent people's safety.

Step 2: Use modal adverbs to express opinions

Modal adverbs show how certain we are about something.

Modal adverbs that show **certainty** include: *definitely, certainly, undoubtedly, surely, absolutely, firmly, strongly, clearly.*

Modal adverbs that show **uncertainty** include: *maybe, perhaps, probably, possibly.*

Using **modal adverbs** helps us express **opinions** by showing **how strongly we feel** about something.

1. In the following sentences, use the word in brackets to help you fill in a suitable **modal adverb** from the lists above. Use a different adverb each time.

   a We could ____________________ try another way of dealing with bullies. (uncertain)

b _______________ we should organise an anti-bullying assembly. (uncertain)

c I _______________ think we need a stronger anti-bullying policy at our school. (certain)

2 Now complete the following sentences by filling in the missing modal adverb and the rest of the sentence.

a _______________ (modal adverb), bullying will only stop being a problem when _______________

b We would _______________ (modal adverb) have fewer wars if _______________

c I _______________ (modal adverb) believe that if people are taught to respect others and their property, _______________

Step 3: Use evaluative language to make judgements

Evaluative language is language that makes positive or negative judgements.
For example: *good, bad.*

Some words are more strongly positive or negative than others.
For example: *Excellent* is more forceful than *good* and *awful* is more forceful than *bad.*

Using evaluative language that makes forceful **positive** or **negative judgements** helps **persuade** your reader or audience that your point of view is right.

1 Arrange the following groups of words from **least forceful** to **most forceful**.

a beautiful breath-taking pretty _______________

b grotesque ugly hideous _______________

c enormous large massive _______________

d gruesome horrible spine-chilling _______________

2 In the following sentences, replace each word in brackets with a more **forceful** alternative from the box. Do not use the same word more than once.

terrible terrified misery destroy unbearable miserable ruin difficult suffering

a People who don't respect others cause a lot of (sadness) _______________ in the world.

b Bullies can make the lives of their victims (unpleasant) _______________.

c The victims of crime are sometimes too (frightened) _______________ to leave their homes.

d Wars can (spoil) _______________ people's lives.

e Many innocent people suffer in these (bad) _______________ wars.

Writing the final draft

This is Angus's **final draft**. Read the comments about his **editorial** on the left, and do the tasks on the right.

Comments

A good **introduction** *captures the reader's attention with an interesting opening sentence. It also* **state***s the main* **opinion**.

Using **modal adverbs** *helps the writer show how certain he or she is about something.*

Linking ideas with ***connectives*** *makes the writing read more fluently.*

Using ***evaluative language*** *helps persuade the reader to accept the writer's point of view.*

A good ***conclusion*** *repeats the main opinion and refers back briefly to the arguments.*

Why it is important to respect the rights of others

Amnesty International is a worldwide organisation that fights to protect human rights. It states that all humans have the right to "basic freedoms and protections". That means that everyone has the right to feel safe. This is not always the case, but I strongly believe that if people learn to respect the rights of others, the world will be a safer place.

People who, for example, do not respect the right of others to be different can become bullies. Bullying is a big problem in many schools. It is also a problem in our school. Children who get picked on can become anxious and lonely and their schoolwork can start to suffer. However, the bullies can also get into serious trouble. I believe that the only way to deal with bullies is to teach them the importance of respecting the rights of others.

People who do not respect the rights of others can also become criminals. Crime is a big problem in our society. Thieves, for instance, take what isn't theirs, while criminals sometimes threaten innocent people's safety.

Crime can ruin the lives of both the criminals and their victims. On the one hand, the victims could end up being too frightened to leave their homes; on the other hand, criminals often have to spend time in prison. If more people learn to respect the rights of others, I am sure we would not have so much crime in the world and people would feel safer.

Finally, if people do not respect the rights of others, it can lead to wars. War causes lots of problems in the world. During wars, innocent people get injured and killed. In addition, they often lose their homes and all their possessions because they are forced to flee. Teaching people to respect the rights of others is clearly the only way to stop wars.

I have given only a few examples of how a lack of respect for the rights of others causes problems in the world. If we can all learn to respect others, no matter how different they are from us, I am certain we can make the world a safer place for everyone.

Tasks

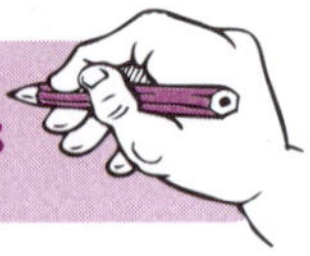

1. **Underline** the sentence that contains the **main opinion**.
2. **Highlight** three **connectives**.
3. **Underline** the **conjunction** that joins two clauses.
4. **Highlight** two **connectives** that show **contrast**.
5. **Circle** the **modal adverb**.
6. **Highlight** the sentence that **refers back** to the arguments.

Student B: Kayla's draft

Kayla, another Year 6 student, is going to write about why it is important to respect the environment. She also starts by organising her thoughts and ideas.

Arguments	Supporting details
Introduction: Pollution—big problem for people, animals, plants—must take better care of environment	
Argument 1: Air pollution (from factories, cars, aeroplanes, power stations) can make people sick	Can cause respiratory diseases, e.g. asthma Can irritate eyes, nose, throat
Argument 2: Water pollution can cause problems for plants, humans and animals	Can cause diseases like typhoid in humans Can kill plants and animals like fish (e.g. plastic bags)
Argument 3: Soil pollution—a problem for plants, humans and animals	Humans, animals eat plants grown in polluted soil—get sick, die Chemicals from landfills go into soil Natural vegetation can die off
Conclusion: Earth is our home—nowhere else to go—have to take better care of it	

1. We can all help reduce air pollution by being more careful in the way we use our cars. List at least two things we can do so that we aren't using our cars unnecessarily.

____

____

____

2. Power stations pollute the air when they burn coal to produce electricity. We can therefore help fight air pollution by reducing the amount of electricity we use. List at least three ways in which we can do this.

____

____

____

____

____

Writing the first draft

This is Kayla's **first draft**. Read what she wrote and then answer the questions.

Why it is important to care for the environment

Pollution is a big problem in the world. We must do something about it.

Air pollution can irritate people's throats, eyes and noses. It can cause respiratory diseases. People can get asthma. Many organisations are trying to find ways to produce clean energy. There are things we can do to help reduce air pollution. We can use our cars less. We can use less electricity. That way we can make a difference.

Water pollution is another problem. Polluted water can give you diseases like typhoid. Polluted water kills plants and fish. People sometimes leave plastic bags lying around. These can end up in streams, rivers and the ocean. Plastic bags can kill fish and turtles. We can help keep our water clean by making sure we always put our rubbish in the bin.

Soil pollution can kill plants and animals and make people sick. Sometimes people use chemicals on plants. They use them to kill insects and weeds. This pollutes the soil. Chemicals from landfills can get into the soil. The chemicals affect plants that grow in the soil. Animals and people that eat the plants can get sick or die.

We need clean air. We need clean water. We need food free from poisons. These are important reasons for taking care of the environment. Earth is our home. We've got nowhere else to go. We must take care of it, mustn't we?

1. Which of these features has Kayla remembered to use in her draft? Tick (✓) the correct answers.
   - a an **opening paragraph** that states the **main opinion** or **point of view** ☐
   - b a series of **arguments** that give **reasons** for the point of view ☐
   - c **evidence** to **support** the **arguments** ☐
   - d **modal verbs** (e.g. *must, can*) ☐
   - e **modal adverbs** (e.g. *definitely, perhaps*) ☐
   - f **present-tense** verbs ☐
   - g **connectives** to link ideas (e.g. *however, for example*) ☐
   - h a separate **paragraph** for each **argument** ☐
   - i **correct spelling** and **punctuation** ☐
   - j a **conclusion** that **repeats** the **main opinion** and **refers back** to the **arguments** ☐

2. Use the information in Kayla's notes and draft to help you complete the following sentences.
   - a People can help reduce air pollution by ______________________________

     ____
   - b Water becomes polluted when ______________________________

     ____

Step-by-step improvement plan

Kayla would also like her **editorial** to appear in the school newspaper, so she is going to do these practice exercises to find ways to improve it. Help her complete them.

Step 1: Start with a good introduction

The **introduction** is the **opening paragraph** of a text. In an **editorial**, it should state the **main opinion**, but it should also be interesting enough to **capture** the reader's **attention** and make him or her want to read further.

Kayla has jotted down some other things she could mention in her introduction.

Pollution—one of biggest problems the world today

Many places—air, water, soil polluted—cause diseases—plants, animals, humans

I believe—must start taking better care of environment—only way to prevent pollution

Now put Kayla's notes together to write a better **introduction** for her **editorial**.

____

____

____

____

Step 2: Writing better sentences

A **sentence** is a group of words that makes complete sense.

For example: *We should always pick up our litter.*

When revising your drafts, try to turn **two or more sentences** into a **single sentence** by **leaving out** or **changing** some of the words.

For example: *Pollution is* ***a big problem. It is one of the biggest problems*** *in the world today.*

Pollution is ***one of the biggest problems*** *in the world today.*

Turning two or more sentences into a single sentence can make your writing tighter and easier to read.

Turn the following sets of sentences into **single sentences**.

1. Air pollution can irritate people's throats, eyes and noses. It can cause respiratory diseases. People can get asthma.

   ____

2. There are things we can do to help reduce air pollution. We can use our cars less. We can use less electricity.

   ____

3. Sometimes people use chemicals on plants. They use them to kill insects and weeds. This pollutes the soil.

   ____

4. Chemicals from landfills can get into the soil. The chemicals affect plants that grow in the soil.

___

5. We need clean air. We need clean water. We need food free from poisons. These are important reasons for taking care of the environment.

___

___

Step 3: Use connectives to link ideas

1. Circle the **connective** that best links the ideas in the following sentences.
   - **a** Pollution can cause many health problems. Air pollution, (instead, nevertheless, for example), can cause respiratory diseases such as asthma.
   - **b** Polluted water contains viruses and bacteria that can kill people. (Therefore, However, Consequently), polluted water (also, too, so) kills plants and animals such as fish.
   - **c** Many organisations are trying to find ways of producing clean energy. (Otherwise, On the one hand, In the meantime), there are things we can do to reduce air pollution.
   - **d** Animals such as fish and turtles die when they get caught in plastic bags or try to eat them; (therefore, instead, in addition) we should never leave our rubbish lying around.
   - **e** We have to start taking better care of the environment; (however, otherwise, moreover) we might end up destroying our planet.
2. Now complete the following sentences.
   - **a** We can help the environment by not using our cars all the time; instead, ___

     ___

     ___
   - **b** Pollution can cause health problems in humans; therefore ___

     ___

     ___

Step 4: Use evaluative language

In the following sentences, circle the option in brackets that sounds **more forceful**.

1. Factories and power stations (spew, send) (harmful, noxious) fumes into the atmosphere.
2. Cars, trucks, trains, ships and aeroplanes also emit (unhealthy, toxic) gases.
3. A (big, large, huge) amount of rubbish ends up in landfills every year.
4. Crops and plants grown in contaminated soil can cause (bad, severe) health problems in humans and animals.
5. A cleaner environment also means a (healthier, better) one.
6. No one wants to live in a (filthy, messy) environment, (full of, thick with) rubbish and (polluted, bad) air.

Writing the final draft

Kayla has started writing the **final draft** of her **editorial**. Help her complete it and then look in the answers section to compare what you have written with what Kayla wrote.

Hint! Look at the practice exercises for ideas.

Why it is important to care for the environment

(Write a good introduction.)

....

....

....

....

....

Air pollution, for example, can cause respiratory diseases such as asthma. It can also irritate people's throats and make their eyes and noses burn. These problems can eventually lead to more serious health issues. Many organisations are trying to find ways of producing clean energy, but in the meantime we can help reduce air pollution by, for example, using less electricity in our homes and using public transport, cycling or walking to school or work. If we all start caring for the environment in a small way, I am convinced we can make a difference.

Water pollution also causes health problems in humans. Polluted water contains viruses and bacteria, and if people drink it they can get diseases such as typhoid. However, polluted water also kills plants and animals such as fish. People often leave their empty packets, cans and bottles lying around outside. Many of these objects, especially plastic bags, end up in streams, rivers and eventually the ocean. Animals die when they get caught in the bags or try to eat them. If we are all more careful about the way we dispose of our waste, I am certain our rivers and oceans will become less polluted.

Finally, soil pollution is a problem for humans, animals and plants. **(Tell how the soil becomes polluted.)** ....

....

....

....

If people and animals eat the plants grown in polluted soil, they can become ill or even die. The chemicals can even destroy the natural vegetation. All of us therefore need to be more careful about the way we care for our plants and dispose of our waste.

The need for clean air, clean water and food free from poisons is obviously an important reason why we should care for the environment. However, we should also remember that Earth is our home. We have nowhere else to go. We therefore have no choice but to look after it.

Your turn

Write an **exposition** of about one or two pages on one of the following. Use your own paper for this activity.

Writing Checklist Make sure your exposition includes: ✓

- an **introduction** that states your **main opinion** or **point of view**. ☐
- a series of **arguments** that give **reasons** for your point of view. ☐
- strong, detailed **evidence** to **support** your **arguments**. ☐
- a separate **paragraph** for each argument. ☐
- **modal verbs** and **adverbs**. ☐
- a variety of **sentences types**. ☐
- **connectives** to link arguments. ☐
- **evaluative** language. ☐
- **correct spelling** and **punctuation**. ☐
- a **conclusion** that **repeats** the **main opinion** and **refers back** to the **arguments**.

Tip Use **Angus's final draft** on page 42 and **Kayla's final draft** on page 47 to help you write your exposition.

Go to WORD BANK page 121 for useful vocabulary

1. Article 12 of the United Nations Convention on the Rights of the Child states:

   > You have the right to give your opinion, and for adults to listen and take it seriously.

   Write an exposition in which you give reasons why it is important for adults to listen to children's opinions and to take them seriously.

2. Article 28 of the United Nations Convention on the Rights of the Child states:

   > You have the right to a good quality education. You should be encouraged to go to school to the highest level you can.

   Write an exposition in which you give reasons why it is important to receive a good education.

3. Which of the following charities would you most likely donate money to? A charity that helps:

   a abandoned pets
   b homeless people
   c old people

   Write an exposition in which you give reasons for your choice.

Unit 5 Explanations

Looking at explanations

An **explanation** is an **informative** text. Its main purpose is to explain **why** or **how** something happens or how it works. The kinds of topics we might write explanations about include the natural world, animal behaviour and technology.

An **explanation** should have:

- an **opening paragraph** that **introduces** the topic with a **general statement** that **describes** or **identifies** the phenomenon.
- a **series** of **paragraphs** that give a sequenced explanation of **how** the phenomenon works or **why** it happens.
- a **conclusion** that either **sums up** the explanation or **wraps it up** in some other way.

Tip! **Diagrams** are often included to support the text.

1. Which of the following texts is an **explanation** of **why** tides occur?

   a The tide was creeping higher and higher up the beach. Soon it would demolish our sandcastle. ☐

   b Tides are caused by the gravitational pull of the moon and sun on the earth's surface. ☐

   c Almost 200 whales have stranded themselves on a New Zealand beach. Rescuers will attempt to refloat them when the next high tide occurs. ☐

2. Look at the following questions. Which four are asking for an **explanation** of **how** something works or **why** it happens?

   a How does a spider spin a web? ☐
   b How big was the spider you saw? ☐
   c How does a plane stay up in the air? ☐
   d What causes an earthquake? ☐
   e Why are you looking up at the sky? ☐
   f Why is the sky blue? ☐

3. The following sentences explain the rain cycle. Number them from 1 to 4 so that they are in the correct sequence.

   a This water vapour then rises into the air. ☐
   b When the water droplets in the clouds are big enough, they can fall as rain. ☐
   c The rain cycle begins when the heat from the sun causes the water from the oceans, rivers and lakes to evaporate and form water vapour. ☐
   d As the water vapour rises higher, it condenses and forms clouds. ☐

Student A: Andrea's draft

Andrea's Year 6 science class is learning about electricity. They have to research and explain how clean sources of energy, such as the sun, wind or water, can be used to produce electricity.

Andrea is going to **explain** how we get electricity from solar energy. She starts by studying the following diagrams.

Andrea also draws a flow chart to help her understand the process of converting sunlight into electricity.

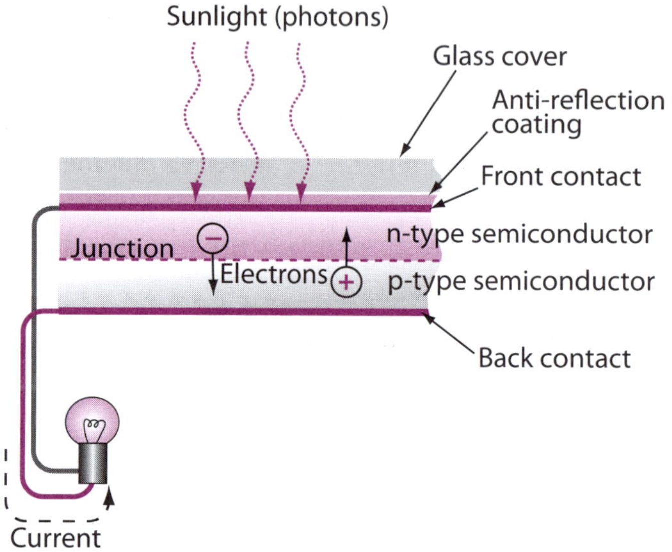

1 panel = many small solar cells → Sunlight hits electrons in solar cells → Electrons start moving → Electric current → Electric circuit → Switches and power points

Flowchart illustrating the conversion of sunlight into electricity

1. Apart from being a clean source of energy, what other advantages are there in using sunlight to produce electricity?

____

____

2. Can you think of any disadvantages in using solar energy to produce electricity?

____

____

____

Writing the first draft

This is Andrea's **first draft**. Read what she wrote, and then answer the questions.

How we get electricity from solar energy

The word *solar* comes from the Latin word *sol*. It means sun. Solar energy is the energy we get from sunlight. All living things need the sun's light to survive.

Special panels called thermal panels turn sunlight into heat. Panels called photovoltaic (PV) panels turn sunlight into electricity. We can capture the sun's light in these special panels. Inside a PV panel are lots of little cells with electrons inside them. In case you didn't know, an electron is a tiny piece of electricity.

The sun's light hits these electrons. This makes other electrons move. Anyway, when these electrons move they create an electric current. Then an electrical circuit captures these currents. From there the electricity goes to switches and power points in our homes and other buildings.

In Australia solar panels should point northwards. That's where the most sunshine comes from in Australia. Solar panels should always point towards the sun. Then they can produce the most power. It's also better to tilt them so that the sun shines right on them.

Producing electricity from sunlight is good for the environment because it doesn't cause pollution.

1 A good **explanation** should contain the following features. Tick (✓) the ones that Andrea has used in her draft.

- **a** an **opening paragraph** that introduces the topic with a **general statement** that **describes** or **identifies** the phenomenon ☐
- **b** a **sequenced explanation** of **how** the phenomenon works or **why** it happens ☐
- **c** **present-tense verbs** (e.g. *comes, makes* or *has*) ☐
- **d** **connectives** or **linking words** that show the **sequence** of **events** (e.g. *First, Next*) ☐
- **e** **conjunctions** and **relative pronouns** to make **compound** and **complex sentences** (e.g. *and, but, because, which*) ☐
- **f** the **passive voice** (e.g. *The sun's light can be captured in special panels and turned into electricity.*) ☐
- **g** **scientific language** (e.g. *photovoltaic cells, electrical circuit*) ☐
- **h** **well-structured paragraphs** that start with a **topic sentence** that tells the reader what the paragraph is about (e.g. *The sun's light can be captured and turned into heat or electricity in special panels.*) ☐
- **i** **correct spelling** and **punctuation** ☐
- **j** a **conclusion** that either **sums up** the **explanation** or **wraps it up** in some other way ☐

2 Explanations should be written in a **formal style**. They should not contain informal expressions like *okay, no way* and *like I said.*

Find two **informal expressions** in paragraphs 2 and 3 and underline them.

Step-by-step improvement plan

Andrea has read over her draft and thinks it is a bit muddled. She also wants it to sound more formal. Help her complete these practice exercises to find ways to do this.

Step 1: Use topic sentences to write well-structured paragraphs

A **topic sentence** is the sentence that contains the **main idea** of a paragraph. It usually appears at the beginning of the paragraph. The other sentences in the paragraph should all relate to the topic sentence in some way.

Starting a paragraph with a topic sentence lets the reader know what the paragraph is about.

For example: **Electricity can be generated in many different ways.** *Most of our electricity is produced by burning fossil fuels such as coal. However, we can also use the power of flowing water, wind and the sun to generate electricity.*

1. In her second paragraph, Andrea explains that thermal panels produce heat and PV panels generate electricity.

   Which of the following sentences would make the best **topic sentence** for the paragraph?

   a Thermal panels capture sunlight and turn it into heat. ☐

   b Photovoltaic (PV) panels capture sunlight and turn it into electricity. ☐

   c Solar panels capture sunlight and turn it into heat or electricity. ☐

2. Carefully read Andrea's third paragraph. What is the **main idea** of this paragraph?

   a How a thermal panel produces heat ☐

   b How a PV panel produces electricity ☐

   c How the switches and power points in our homes work ☐

Step 2: Use conjunctions and relative pronouns to write better sentences

In Unit 2 you learned that there are three types of sentences: **simple sentences**, which contain **one main clause**; **compound sentences**, which contain **two main clauses**; and **complex sentences**, which contain a **main clause** and a **subordinate clause**.

For example: *Solar panels* **capture** *sunlight.* (simple sentence—one main clause)

Solar panels **capture** *sunlight and* **turn** *it into heat or electricity.* (compound sentence—two main clauses)

Solar panels, which **turn** *sunlight into heat and electricity,* **are placed** *on roofs.* (complex sentence—one main clause and one subordinate clause)

Reminder! **Compound sentences** are formed by joining two clauses with the **conjunctions** *and, or, but* or *so*. **Complex sentences** are formed by joining two clauses with the **relative pronouns** *who, whose, which* or *that*, or **conjunctions** like *because, before, if, when, while, unless* or *until.*

Using a variety of sentence types makes your writing more interesting to read.

Use either a **conjunction** or a **relative pronoun** to turn each of the following pairs of sentences into a single sentence.

1. The word *solar* comes from the Latin word *sol.* It means sun. ______________________

____

2. Solar energy is the energy we get from sunlight. All living things need the sun's light to survive. ______________________

____

3. The panels that produce heat are called thermal panels. The panels that generate electricity are called photovoltaic (PV) panels. ______________________

____

Step 3: Use the passive voice

Verbs can be either **active** or **passive.** They are active when the subject of the sentence does the action, and they are passive when the subject of the sentence has the action done to them.

For example: *Solar panels capture sunlight.* (active voice)
Sunlight is captured in solar panels. (passive voice)

We use the **passive voice** when we are more interested in the **process** than in the person or thing responsible for the process. Usually when we start using the passive voice we continue with it. However, sometimes the passive voice makes sentences more difficult to understand and it is better to use the active voice.

1. Rewrite the following sentences in the **passive voice**. You have been given the first few words in each case.

   a. We can turn sunlight into heat and electricity.

      Sunlight can ______________________

   b. An electrical circuit captures the electric currents.

      The electric currents are ______________________

      ____

   c. You should tilt solar panels at an angle.

      Solar panels should ______________________

2. The following sentences have been written in the passive voice and sound clumsy. Rewrite them in the **active voice**. You have been shown how to start each sentence.

   a. Major advantages are to be had from using solar energy to produce electricity.

      Using solar energy ______________________

      ____

   b. Air pollution is not caused when electricity is produced from solar energy.

      Producing electricity from solar energy ______________________

Writing the final draft

This is Andrea's **final draft**. Read the comments about her **explanation** on the left, and do the tasks on the right.

Comments

Starting with a **general statement** *that introduces the topic prepares the reader for what is to come.*

Using **scientific language** *gives the explanation a sense of authority.*

Using the **passive voice** *in moderation focuses attention on the process rather than the person or thing responsible for the process.*

Starting each **paragraph** *with a* **topic sentence** *helps the reader make sense of the explanation.*

Outlining *the advantages and disadvantages of using solar energy to produce electricity helps to wrap up the explanation.*

How we get electricity from solar energy

The word *solar* comes from the Latin word *sol*, which means sun. Solar energy is therefore the energy we get from sunlight, which every living thing needs to survive.

The sun's energy can be harnessed in special panels and converted into heat and electricity that we can use in our homes. The panels that produce heat are called thermal panels, while those that generate electricity are called photovoltaic (PV) panels. Each PV panel is made up of many small cells that contain electrons (tiny pieces of electricity).

Electricity starts forming when light from the sun hits an electron in the PV panel. This causes other electrons to move, creating an electric current. These currents are then captured in an electrical circuit, which delivers electricity to switches and power points in our homes and other buildings.

To work really well, solar panels need to capture as much sunlight as possible, so they should always point towards the sun. In Australia, that means they should face northwards. They should also be tilted so that they face directly towards the sun.

Using solar energy to produce electricity has three big advantages: it does not pollute the air, it is a renewable source of energy and it is free. However, two of the big problems with using the sun's energy to make electricity are that there are many places on Earth that do not get much sunshine, and the sun does not shine for 24 hours every day. Scientists therefore need to find a way to capture and store the sun's energy so that it can be used in different places and at different times.

Tasks

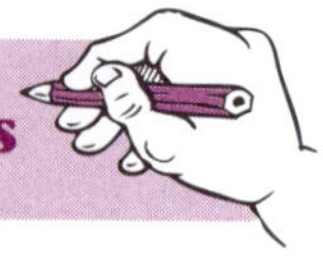

1. **Highlight** a **relative pronoun**.
2. **Underline** the words that are **similar in meaning** to *captured, turned* and *produce*.
3. **Highlight** a clause that is in the **passive voice**.
4. **Circle** the **conjunction**.
5. **Highlight** two **connectives**.

Student B: Dev's draft

Dev, another Year 6 student, is going to explain how we get electricity from wind power. He starts by studying the following diagrams.

Dev also draws a flow chart to help him understand the process of converting wind energy into electricity.

Wind turbine

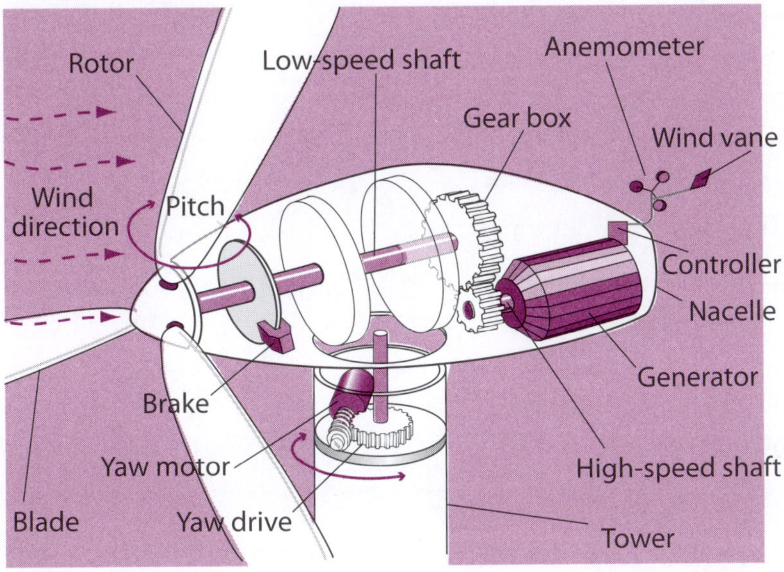

Wind turns rotors (blades) → Drive shaft turns slowly–16 rpm → Gear box increases speed–1600 rpm
↓
Drives generator → moves electrons in magnets inside wire coils → Electric current starts to flow

Flowchart illustrating the process of converting wind energy

1 List at least one way in which we use the wind's energy:

a in and around our homes. ______________________

b on farms. ______________________

c on the water. ______________________

2 The first two processes in the flow chart could be written as a single sentence as follows: *Wind turns the rotors, which cause the drive shaft to turn slowly.*

Now write the last two processes as a **single sentence**. Start like this:

The generator causes ______________________

____

____

Writing the first draft

This is Dev's **first draft**. Read what he wrote and then answer the questions.

How we get electricity from wind energy

The wind can move boats and ships. It can cool down our homes and buildings. It can turn windmills to pump water and grind grain. People have been using the wind's energy for centuries.

Wind turbines are large machines on very tall towers. Wind turbines have three rotors or blades. When the wind blows, it turns the rotors. Then the drive shaft starts to turn slowly. It only does 16 revolutions per minute. Then a gearbox makes the drive shaft turn faster. Now it does 1600 rpm. This is fast enough to make the generator behind the gearbox work.

There are coils of wire with magnets in them on the drive shaft. The electrons in the magnets start moving. This causes an electric current.

Energy companies build wind farms in windy places. Wind farms are really big because you need lots of turbines to make enough electricity for homes and other buildings.

Using wind power to make electricity doesn't cause air pollution. Using wind power to make electricity is better than using fossil fuels. It is also renewable. But some people don't like wind farms. They say they are ugly and noisy.

1. Which of these features has Dev remembered to include in his draft? Tick (✓) the ones that he has used.

   a an **opening paragraph** that introduces the topic with a **general statement** that **describes** or **identifies** the phenomenon ☐

   b a **sequenced explanation** of **how** the phenomenon works or **why** it happens ☐

   c **present-tense verbs** ☐

   d **connectives** or **linking words** that show the **sequence** of **events** ☐

   e **conjunctions** and **relative pronouns** to make **compound** and **complex sentences** ☐

   f **passive voice** ☐

   g **scientific language** ☐

   h **well-structured paragraphs** that start with a **topic sentence** that tells the reader what the paragraph is about ☐

   i **correct spelling** and **punctuation** ☐

   j a **conclusion** that either **sums up** the **explanation** or **wraps it up** in some other way ☐

2. Choose the best word or phrase to replace each of the following in Dev's draft.

a	cool down (paragraph 1)	refrigerate	☐	ventilate	☐	reduce	☐
b	turn (paragraph 2)	circle	☐	whirl	☐	rotate	☐
c	to make work (paragraph 2)	to drive	☐	to push	☐	to transport	☐

Step-by-step improvement plan

Dev also wants to make improvements to his draft, so he is going to do some practice exercises to find ways to do this. Help him complete them.

Step 1: Use topic sentences to write well-structured paragraphs

1 Carefully read the following short paragraph.

> Electricity is produced mainly by power stations that burn coal. It can also be produced by wind turbines, solar panels, nuclear power, fast-flowing water and batteries.

Which of the following would make the best **topic sentence** for the paragraph?

a Electricity has been an important part of our lives for just over a century. ☐

b There are many different ways of producing electricity. ☐

c When electrons move, they carry electrical energy from one place to another. ☐

2 Dev's **explanation** is a bit muddled because he hasn't started his paragraphs with a **topic sentence**.

a Reread Dev's opening paragraph. Underline the sentence that should come at the beginning.

b Look at Dev's second paragraph. Which of the following would make the best **topic sentence** for this paragraph?

The wind's energy can be turned into electricity using turbines. ☐

Wind turbines are very powerful machines. ☐

Wind turbines have blades that turn when the wind blows. ☐

Step 2: Use conjunctions and relative pronouns to write better sentences

Dev's sentences would flow better if he joined some of them with conjunctions or relative pronouns.

Use **conjunctions** and **relative pronouns** to turn the following sentences into **single sentences**.

Reminder! You will have to leave out some words in the final sentence.

1 For centuries, people have been using the wind's energy to move ships across rivers and oceans. They have been using it to ventilate their homes and buildings.

____

____

____

2. They have built windmills. Windmills have allowed them to grind grain. Windmills have allowed them to pump water mechanically. ______________________

3. More recently, people have started harnessing the wind's energy in a turbine. A turbine is a machine. It spins around in a fast-moving flow of air, steam, gas, water or other fluid.

4. The magnets inside the coils of wire start to move. Electrons break free from the metal. They start to flow. ______________________

5. Many people think that wind farms are ugly. They think that they spoil the landscape. Some people who live close to wind farms complain of the noise emitted by the turbine.

Step 3: Use the passive voice

Some of Dev's sentences would be better if he wrote them in the passive voice.

1. Rewrite the following sentences in the **passive voice**. In each case, you have been given the first few words.

   a People can harness the wind's energy to produce electricity.

   The wind's energy can ______________________

   b People convert the wind's energy into electricity in large machines called turbines.

   The wind's energy is ______________________

   c People mount wind turbines on very tall towers.

   Wind turbines are ______________________

   d You need lots of turbines to generate enough electricity to power people's homes and other buildings.

   Lots of turbines are ______________________

2. Now use Dev's draft to help you complete the following sentence.

   The generator behind the gearbox is driven ______________________

Writing the final draft

Dev has started writing the **final draft** of his **explanation**. Help him complete it and then look in the answers section to compare what you have written with what Dev wrote.

Hint! Look at Dev's first draft and practice exercises for ideas.

How we get electricity from wind energy

People have been using the wind's energy for centuries. They have used it to move ships across rivers and oceans and to ventilate homes and other buildings. They have also built windmills that allowed them to grind grain and pump water mechanically—tasks that windmills perform to this day.

More recently, the wind's energy has been harnessed to produce electricity. This is done using a turbine, which is a machine that spins around in a fast-moving flow of air (such as on a windmill), steam, gas, water or other fluid.

(Rewrite Dev's second paragraph, giving it a topic sentence, combining some of the sentences with conjunctions or relative pronouns and adding more detail where necessary.)

On the rotating shaft in the gearbox are magnets and coils of wire. When the magnets inside the coils of wire are moved, electrons (tiny pieces of electricity) break free from the metal and start to flow, resulting in an electric current.

(Conclude by discussing the positives and negatives of using wind energy to generate electricity.)

Your turn

Write an **explanation** of about one to two pages on one of the following. Use your own paper for this activity.

Writing Checklist Make sure your explanation contains: ✓

- an **opening paragraph** that **introduces** the topic with a **general statement** that **describes** or **identifies** the phenomenon. ☐
- a **sequenced explanation** of **how** the phenomenon works or **why** it happens. ☐
- **present-tense verbs**. ☐
- **scientific language**. ☐
- **well-structured paragraphs** that start with a **topic sentence** that tells the reader what the paragraph is about. ☐
- **correct spelling** and **punctuation**. ☐
- a **conclusion** that either **sums up** the **explanation** or **wraps it up** in some other way. ☐

Tip Use **Andrea's final draft** on page 54 and **Dev's final draft** on page 59 to help you write your explanation.

Go to WORD BANK pages 121–122 for useful vocabulary

1. Use the following diagram and notes to help you explain how a simple electric circuit works.

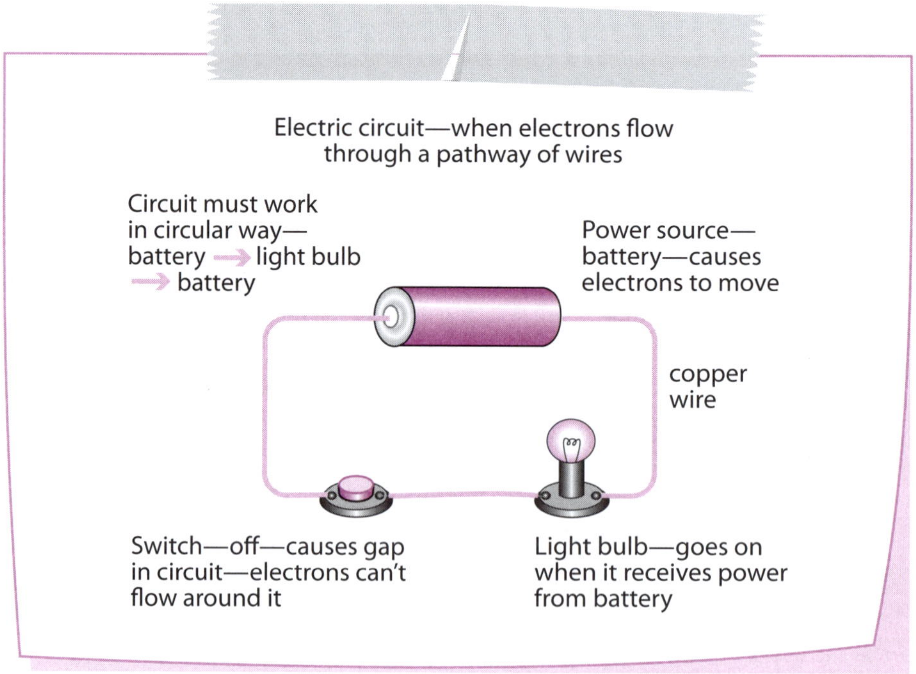

2. Research hydroelectricity (the generation of electricity using flowing water) and explain how it works.

3. Explain how something you know well works; for example, how a caterpillar turns into a butterfly, how bees make honey or how your favourite computer game works.

Unit 6 Narratives

Looking at narratives

A **narrative** tells a story based on a real or imagined event. Its main **purpose** is to **entertain**, but many narratives are **informative** and may even contain important **lessons about life**. Fantasies, for example, often depict the struggle between good and evil, with good winning out in the end.

Most **narratives** have:

- a **hook** (usually the opening paragraph) to draw the reader in.
- an **orientation** that sets the scene, usually by telling **who**, **what**, **where** and **when**.
- a **complication** or **problem** that has to be solved, usually by the main character.
- a **series** of **events** that result from the complication.
- an **ending** or **resolution**, in which the problem is solved.

1. There are many different categories or genres of **narrative**. Choose three that you like to write about.

Adventure ☐	Fairy tale ☐	Fantasy ☐	Historical fiction ☐
Horror ☐	Humour ☐	Legend ☐	Mystery ☐
Myth ☐	Real life ☐	Science fiction ☐	

2. Read the following lines from narratives and match them to the **genres** listed above.

Hint! Each text may fall under more than one genre; for example, real life and adventure.

a As soon as Jemma swallowed the potion her skin started to change colour. It became paler and paler until she disappeared altogether. Yes! She had done it! She had become invisible.

____

b Although he was the son of a Titan, Prometheus did not live with the rest of the gods on Mount Olympus. He chose, instead, to live among the humans. Prometheus found them shivering from cold and almost starving to death. He decided to help the humans by asking Zeus, chief of the gods, to give them the gift of fire.

____

c The colonists had been on Mars for ten years now and thanks to all the trees they had planted the oxygen levels on the planet were continuing to rise. Soon they would be able to leave the safety of their dome-like structures without first having to don a spacesuit.

____

3. Now choose a suitable **title** for each of the texts in question 2.

a ______________________

b ______________________

c ______________________

Student A: Danny's draft

Danny's Year 6 class is reading the novel *The Hobbit*, by JRR Tolkien.
It's a **fantasy** story about a little hobbit, Bilbo Baggins, who accompanies a group of dwarves on a quest to reclaim the kingdom of Erebor. Along the way Bilbo has many adventures and has to overcome many challenges, all of which help him grow as a person.

Danny's class has been discussing some of the challenges children have to face as part of the process of growing up. These are some of the ideas they have come up with.

learning to walk

going to school for the first time

sleeping away from home for the first time

learning to ride a bicycle

going on your first school camp

changing schools

learning to share

not getting picked for a team

Now the students have to choose one of the ideas on the board and build a narrative around it.

Danny is going to write about a boy who overcame his fear of learning to ride a bicycle. He starts by planning his **narrative**.

Hook—Tom confronts the bicycle in the shed—calls it the "beast"

Who? Tom, Dad, Grandpa

What? Tom gets bicycle for his birthday

Where? Tom's house—shed

When? 8 years old

Problem/complication—Tom can't ride a bicycle—boys laugh at him—won't go near his new bike

Series of events—Tom hears Grandpa and Dad talking—Grandpa surprised

Tom can't ride bike—Dad's comment upsets Tom—makes Tom determined to learn—takes bike onto driveway—tries to ride it—keeps trying

Resolution—Finally gets it right!

1. Imagine Tom wanted to show his dad and grandpa that he could ride a bike. What might he have said to them?

____

____

2. What might Tom's grandpa have said when he saw him riding the bike?

____

____

3. What might Tom's dad have said? ______________________________

____

Writing the first draft

This is Danny's **first draft**. Read what he wrote and then answer the questions.

Tom learns to ride a bike

Tom's friend Jett got a bike for his birthday. Jett let everyone ride it at his party. Everyone could ride a bike except for Tom. He kept falling off and the other boys made fun of him. He was very embarrassed and didn't like bicycles after that.

Then Tom got a bike when he turned eight. His dad was excited to show it to him. It was in the shed. Tom remembered how the boys had teased him at Jett's party, so he just looked at it and wouldn't go anywhere near it. His dad was disappointed.

Then one morning two months later Tom heard Grandpa and Dad talking. Grandpa thought it was bad that Tom was eight years old and couldn't ride a bike. Dad said they gave him one for his birthday but he was scared of it. That did it! Tom made up his mind—he was going to learn to ride that bike! He put on his helmet and went to the shed to get it.

He practised on the driveway. The first time he tried he fell off. He tried again and fell off. This went on for quite some time. He was full of bruises, scrapes and scratches, but he wouldn't give up. He tried and tried and tried.

After trying thousands of times, he eventually learnt to keep his balance. He could finally ride a bike! He had overcome his fear.

1 A good **narrative** should contain the following features. Tick (✓) the ones that Danny has used in his draft.

- **a** a **hook** that draws the reader in ☐
- **b** an **orientation** that tells **who**, **what**, **where** and **when** ☐
- **c** a **complication** or **problem** that has to be solved ☐
- **d** a **series** of **events**, divided into paragraphs ☐
- **e** a **resolution** that shows how the problem is solved and **wraps up** the story ☐
- **f** **past-tense verbs** (e.g. *heard, practised*) ☐
- **g** **descriptive verbs** (e.g. *gleamed, tormented*) ☐
- **h** **figurative language** (e.g. *The bicycle was a beast that had to be conquered.*) ☐
- **i** interesting **information** and **detail** about the events ☐
- **j** **correct spelling** and **punctuation** ☐

2 If Danny were to add some dialogue to his narrative, what might Grandpa's exact words have been?

- **a** "Eight years old and he can't ride a bike yet!" ☐
- **b** "There are some eight-year-olds who can't ride a bike." ☐
- **c** "I couldn't ride a bike when I was eight years old." ☐

Step-by-step improvement plan

Danny is not happy with his first draft, so he is going to do some work on it to make it more interesting and entertaining. Help him complete these practice exercises to find ways to do this.

Step 1: Add colour with figurative language

Figurative language includes **figures of speech** like **similes**, **metaphors** and **personification**, which you learnt about in Unit 3.

Reminder!

- A **simile** compares two things that are unlike each other, using the words *like* or *as*.
  For example: *The wheels were* **like** *two big eyes. I was* **as** *happy* **as** *a dog with a bone.*
- A **metaphor** makes a more direct comparison between two unlike things, without using the words *like* or *as*.
  For example: *The bike was a scary monster.*
- **Personification** is a type of metaphor in which animals and objects are given human qualities.
  For example: *The bike stared at me, challenging me to ride it.*

Adding similes, metaphors and personification will make Danny's narrative more interesting to read.

1 Danny has written down some things he could **compare** Tom's bike and helmet to. Circle the best option in each case.

Bike—an animal, a beast, an alien

Helmet—a shell, an umbrella, a canopy

2 Complete each of the following sentences with a **simile**. Use the comparisons above to help you.

a The bike stood at the back of the shed, ______________________

b The helmet was as snug as ______________________

3 What might Danny **compare** Tom's injuries to? Choose the better option in each case.

a a bruise on his leg — a bright green leaf ☐ — a dark purple flower ☐

b scrapes and scratches on his knees and elbows — paintings ☐ — scribbles ☐

4 Now write two interesting sentences about Tom's injuries. Use the comparisons in question 3 to help you include a **metaphor** in each sentence.

a ______________________

____

b ______________________

____

5. If the bicycle were given human qualities, which of the following actions could it be doing? Choose the three best options.

a winking at Tom ☐	**b** crying bitterly ☐	**c** mocking Tom ☐
d yelling at Tom ☐	**e** laughing at Tom ☐	**f** helping Tom ☐

Step 2: Add interest with descriptive verbs

In Unit 3 you also learned that some verbs are more useful than others because they **describe** exactly **how an action is performed**. For example, *I* **folded** *my fingers around the handlebars* is more descriptive than *I* **put** *my fingers around the handlebars* because it shows exactly how the action was performed.

Using **descriptive verbs** adds interest to your writing.

Danny needs to find a more **descriptive verb** to replace each underlined one in the following sentences. Help him choose the most descriptive verbs from the box.

troubled	encouraged	tormented	leaning
glowing	lounging	gleaming	spurred

1. The beast was <u>standing</u> ____________________ against the back wall.
2. Sparks of light were <u>shining</u> ____________________ on its silver handlebars.
3. Dad's words <u>hurt</u> ____________________ Tom all day.
4. Dad's words <u>moved</u> ____________________ Tom into action.

Step 3: Add variety with short and long sentences

A **sentence** is a group of words that makes complete sense, even if it consists of only three words.

For example: *The bike wobbled.*

In a narrative, using a series of **short sentences** helps to create a **sense** of **excitement**.

For example: *Tom positioned himself on the saddle. He kept his left foot on the ground. He pushed down on the pedal with his right foot. Suddenly he was moving forward!*

Longer sentences, on the other hand, flow better and allow you to include more **detail**.

For example: *He positioned himself on the saddle and, keeping his left foot on the ground, pushed down on the pedal with his right foot.*

Using a **mixture** of **short** and **long sentences** adds **variety** to your narrative and stops your reader from getting bored.

1. Write the following short sentences as **one long sentence**.

   Dad's words tormented Tom all day. They were like a thorn festering inside his flesh. They spurred him into action. ____

   ____

2. Now write the following long sentence as **three short sentences**.

   He was balanced and in control and the bike was obeying him. ____________________

   ____

Writing the final draft

This is Danny's **final draft**. Read the comments about his narrative on the left, and do the tasks on the right.

Comments

An interesting **opening paragraph** *acts as a* **hook** *that draws the reader in.*

Using **descriptive verbs** *adds interest to your writing.*

Using a variety of **short** *and* **long sentences** *makes your writing more interesting to read.*

Using **dialogue** *brings your characters to life.*

Using **figurative language** *helps your reader visualise what is being described.*

Using a **series** *of* **short sentences** *helps build excitement.*

A good **conclusion** *provides a satisfying ending.*

Conquering the beast

Tom walked into the shed, his helmet snug on his head. The beast was lounging against the back wall, sparks of light gleaming on its silver handlebars, like eyes winking at him, mocking him.

Two months ago Tom's father, beaming from ear to ear, had led him to this very same shed. "Happy birthday, son!" he'd exclaimed, as he removed the sheet from the object it was covering. Tom's heart had sunk. In front of him was a bicycle. In his head he heard the voices of the boys at Jett's party making fun of him because he couldn't ride Jett's new bike. He'd tried, but each time he'd fallen off and hurt himself. He'd never felt so humiliated, and it was the bike's fault! So when his father had presented him with this one on his eighth birthday, he'd stubbornly refused to go anywhere near it.

"Eight years old and he can't ride a bike yet!" he'd heard Grandpa exclaim that morning. But it was his father's reply that really stung him: "We got him a bike for his birthday, but he's terrified of it, like it's a beast or something." Dad's words tormented him all day, like a thorn festering inside his flesh, but they also spurred him into action. He would show them. He would conquer the beast.

Tom took two determined strides towards the bike. He folded his fingers firmly around the rubber grips on the handlebars and wheeled it out of the shed and onto the driveway. "It won't bite you," he told himself, as he prepared to launch his first attack.

Carefully he positioned himself on the saddle. With his left foot still on the ground, he gently pushed down on the pedal with his right foot. As he started to move forward he brought up his left foot. The bike wobbled and … crash! He was on the ground, the bicycle on top of him. He got up and tried again, and again, and again. A bruise was blossoming on his leg, and scrapes and scratches formed little scribbles on his knees and elbows, but he kept on trying.

And then the moment of victory! On what seemed like his thousandth attempt, his left foot joined his right foot on the pedals and something clicked into place. He was balanced. The bike was obeying him. He had conquered the beast!

Tasks

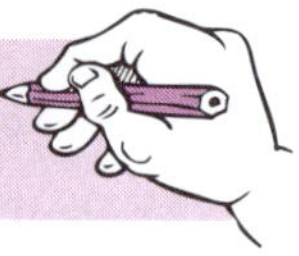

1. **Highlight** the **simile**.
2. **Circle** the word that is **similar in meaning** to *embarrassed*.
3. **Underline** the **metaphor**.
4. **Highlight** the **adverb** (a word that tells how, where or when something is done).
5. **Underline** two **metaphors**.
6. **Highlight** the sentences that help **build excitement**.

Student B: Aisha's draft

Aisha, another Year 6 student, is going to build her narrative around the challenge of having to change schools.

She also starts by planning her **narrative**.

Hook—Lucinda's feelings when she arrives at her new school

Who? Lucinda, Mum, Alex, Miss Roberts

What? Lucinda's first day at her new school

Where? the new school

Problem/complication—Mum got a promotion—they had to move to another city—Lucinda upset—had to change schools

Series of events—Lucinda is anxious—Alex comes up to her—introduces her to other students—friendly—L worries about meeting new teacher—kind, caring—L likes her

Resolution—First day at new school not as bad as she'd feared—L starts looking forward to her new life

1. Complete the following sentence with the **exact words** Mum might have used. Remember to use the correct **punctuation**.

   One day Mum came home from work looking excited. She said to Lucinda,

2. What might Lucinda have said when she heard about Mum's promotion?

   Lucinda's face fell. She said,

3. What might Miss Roberts have said when she introduced Lucinda to the class?

   Miss Roberts said,

4. Write two sentences describing how you would feel if you had to change schools.

Writing the first draft

This is Aisha's **first draft**. Read what she wrote and then answer the questions.

The new school

Lucinda walked through the gates of her new school. She was really nervous. She wanted to hold Mum's hand. She looked at the other kids on the playground. They all knew each other. Suddenly she felt very lonely.

Not so long ago things had been different. She'd been so happy at her old school. But then one day her mother said that she'd been promoted and they'd be moving to another city. Mum was very excited, but Lucinda wasn't.

The thing Lucinda had worried about most was going to a new school. As she stood on the playground with Mum, lots of questions went through her head. Would the other students like her? Would her teachers like her? Would she like them? Then a tall girl with dark hair came up to her. She said her name was Alex and she asked Lucinda to come and meet some of the other students.

Lucinda followed Alex to one of the groups she'd seen earlier. They were friendly. She started to feel better. Then she remembered she still had to meet her new teacher. Her new teacher's name was Miss Roberts. She was kind and caring and Lucinda liked her a lot.

Finally the home time bell rang. Lucinda had made it through the first day at her new school. It hadn't been so bad. Maybe everything would be all right after all.

1. Which of these features has Aisha remembered to include in her draft? Tick (✓) the correct answers.

   a a **hook** that draws the reader in ☐

   b an **orientation** that tells **who**, **what**, **where** and **when** ☐

   c a **complication/problem** that has to be solved ☐

   d a **series** of **events**, divided into paragraphs ☐

   e **past-tense verbs** ☐

   f **descriptive verbs** ☐

   g **figurative language** ☐

   h interesting **information** and **detail** about the events ☐

   i **correct spelling** and **punctuation** ☐

   j a **resolution** that shows how the problem is solved and **wraps up** the story ☐

2. Use the information in Aisha's draft to complete the following sentences.

   a Lucinda felt sad when ______________________________

   ____

   b When Mum asked Lucinda about her new school, Lucinda said, ______________________________

   ____

   ____

Step-by-step improvement plan

Aisha also wants to make her narrative more interesting and is going to do some practice exercises to find ways to do this. Help her complete them.

Step 1: Add colour with figurative language

1. Circle the option in brackets that best completes each sentence. Write down whether the figure of speech is a **simile** or a **metaphor**.

   a Lucinda was as nervous as a (bull, kitten, giraffe) as she walked through the gates of her new school. ______________

   b Lucinda looked nervously at the (carpet, field, sea) of strange faces in front of her. ______________

   c Lucinda was so nervous her legs felt like (jelly, plastic, wood). ______________

2. Write an interesting sentence about Lucinda with each of the following comparisons. The comparison may be a **simile** or a **metaphor**.

the new school—alien territory	the feeling of not belonging—a fish out of water	Lucinda's reaction to the move—her world fell apart

   a ____

   ____

   b ____

   ____

   c ____

   ____

Step 2: Add interest with descriptive verbs

1. Aisha has found more interesting **verbs** to replace some of those in her draft. The verbs in each set have a similar meaning. Look back at Aisha's draft before circling the one you think Aisha should use.

hold (paragraph 1)	grasp, clutch, clench
worried about (paragraph 3)	dreaded, feared, fretted
went (paragraph 3)	rushed, tumbled, raced
seen (paragraph 5)	glimpsed, noticed, spotted

2. Aisha wants to add the following sentences to her narrative, but she isn't sure which **verbs** to use. Help her choose the more descriptive one in each case.

   a She (cast, directed) her eyes nervously around the playground.

   b Students were (standing, gathered) in little clusters.

c A friendly voice (cut, broke) into her thoughts.

d Lucinda was so (wrapped, caught) up in her own little world she didn't (see, notice) a tall girl with dark hair approaching her.

e As she thought of her new life, a little quiver of excitement (moved, raced) up her spine.

3 Use the **descriptive verbs** in brackets to write two more interesting sentences that Aisha could use in her narrative.

a (trembled) ______________________________

____

b (mumbled) ______________________________

____

Step 3: Add variety with short and long sentences

1 Rewrite each of the following short sentences as a **single, longer sentence**. You have been shown how to start each sentence.

a She looked at the other kids on the playground. They all knew each other. Suddenly she felt very lonely.

All the other kids on the playground ______________________________

____

b Now Lucinda stood on the playground. A string of questions tumbled through her head.

Now, as Lucinda ______________________________

____

c She was completely wrapped up in her own little world. She didn't notice a tall girl with dark hair approaching her. A friendly voice cut into her thoughts.

She was so ______________________________

____

d Lucinda needn't have worried. Her teacher was kind and caring. Lucinda liked her immediately.

However, ______________________________

____

2 Now write each of the following long sentences as **three short sentences**.

a The knot in her stomach grew tighter and her legs felt like jelly because this was unknown territory.

____

____

b Lucinda asked herself lots of questions, like would the other students like her and would she like them.

____

____

Writing the final draft

Aisha has started writing the **final draft** of her **narrative**. Help her complete it and then look in the answers section to compare what you have written with what Aisha wrote.

Hint! Look at Aisha's first draft and practice exercises for ideas.

The New School

Lucinda wanted to clutch her mum's hand as they walked through the gates, but she didn't dare. She cast her eyes nervously around the playground. Students were gathered in little clusters, talking and laughing happily together. The knot in her stomach grew tighter. Her legs felt like jelly. This was unknown territory, and she was the alien.

Not so long ago things had been different. **(Continue the paragraph, describing Lucinda's reaction when Mum said they'd be moving to another city.)**

....

....

....

....

The thing Lucinda had dreaded the most about their move was going to a new school. Now, as she stood on the playground, a string of questions tumbled through her head. Would the other students like her? Would her teachers like her? Would she like them?

She was so wrapped up in her own little world that she didn't notice a tall girl with dark hair approaching her. A friendly voice cut into her thoughts. **(Write down Alex's exact words to Lucinda.)**

....

....

Lucinda quickly said goodbye to her mum and followed Alex to one of the groups she'd spotted earlier. Alex introduced her to the other students in the group. They smiled at her and asked her questions about her old school. **(Continue the paragraph, describing Lucinda's fears about meeting her new teacher and how she felt when she met Miss Roberts.)**

....

....

....

When the home time bell rang at three o'clock, Lucinda breathed a sigh of relief. She'd made it through the first day, and it hadn't been as bad as she'd feared. She liked her teacher, she liked the school, and she'd even made some new friends. **(Complete this paragraph, describing Lucinda's feelings about the future.)**

....

....

....

....

Your turn

Write a **narrative** of one to two pages on one of the following. Use your own paper for this activity.

Writing Checklist Make sure your narrative contains: ✓

- a **hook** that draws the reader in. ☐
- an **orientation** that sets the scene by telling **who**, **what**, **where** and **when**. ☐
- a **problem** or **complication** that has to be solved. ☐
- **a series** of **events**, divided into paragraphs. ☐
- **past-tense verbs**. ☐
- **descriptive verbs**. ☐
- **figurative language**. ☐
- **interesting information** and **detail** about the events. ☐
- **correct spelling** and **punctuation**. ☐
- a **resolution** that shows how the problem is solved and **wraps up** the story. ☐

Tip Use **Danny's final draft** on page 66 and **Aisha's final draft** on page 71 to help you write your narrative.

Go to WORD BANK page 122 for useful vocabulary

1. Build a narrative around one of the following situations. You may change the characters' names if you wish.
   a. Savannah accidentally gets locked in a small, dark room. Write about how it happened, how Savannah reacted and how the problem was resolved.
   b. Flynn has left his schoolbag, containing most of his school books and his collection of trading cards, on the bus. Write about how it happened, how Flynn reacted and how the problem was resolved.
   c. Sul, the most inquisitive elf at Elven School, accidentally swallows the wrong potion. Write about how it happened, how Sul was affected by the potion and how the problem was resolved.
   d. Napol and Duggal, two young astronauts from Zardok, accidentally land their spaceship on the wrong planet. Write about how it happened, their experiences on the planet and how the problem was resolved.

2. Build a situation around one of these pictures and then write a narrative about it.

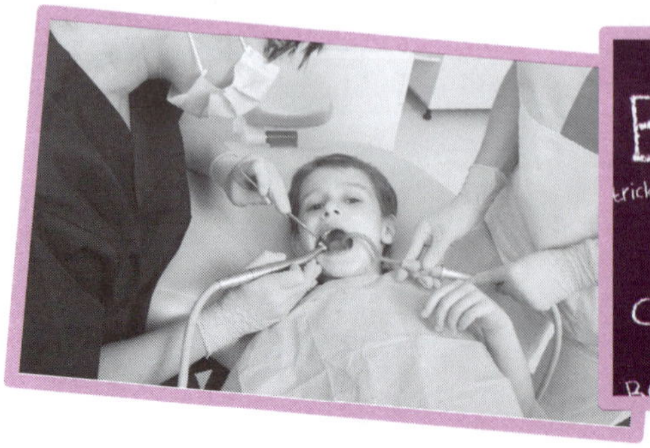

Unit 7 Poetry—free verse poems

Looking at free verse poems

A **poem** is a text that **expresses ideas** or **describes** people and things in an **imaginative** way. **Poetry** is generally meant to be spoken or read aloud, so poets often make use of sound patterns such as **repetition**, **onomatopoeia** and **alliteration**.

The main aim of poetry is to get an **emotional response**, such as joy or sadness, from the reader or listener. However, it also aims to **entertain** or **amuse**.

Unlike most poems, **free verse poems** do not have a rhyme pattern and do not need to have a regular rhythm. However, they have a greater sense of rhythm than other imaginative texts, such as narratives.

A **free verse poem:**

- is usually arranged in **stanzas**, with irregular line breaks.
- uses language that **shows**, rather than tells.

  For example: *Perspiration trickled down Rick's neck.* (This shows that Rick was feeling hot.)

1 Which of the following texts is an example of a **free verse poem**?

a Is the moon tired?
She looks so pale
Within her misty veil:
She scales the sky
From east to west,
And takes no rest. ☐

b There was a table set out under a tree in front of the house, and the March Hare and the Hatter were having tea at it: a Dormouse was sitting between them, fast asleep, and the other two were using it as a cushion, resting their elbows on it, and talking over its head. "Very uncomfortable for the Dormouse," thought Alice; "only, as it's asleep, I suppose it doesn't mind." ☐

c A noiseless patient spider
stood isolated.
Exploring its surroundings
it launched forth filament,
filament, filament,
out of itself. ☐

2 Rewrite the following **free verse poem** as though it were part of a **narrative**. Use **correctly punctuated sentences** and change the **verbs** to the **past tense**; e.g. *tossed* instead of *tosses*. Make any other changes you think are necessary.

The rain falls hard today
The leaves are wet, the clouds are heavy
Above the earth; on the river bank the ferns
Gleam in the faint light; the river tosses and swirls
Rolling relentlessly across the open plain.

Student A: Raoul's draft

Raoul's Year 6 class have been learning about free verse poetry.
Now each student has to write his or her own **free verse poem**.

Before he starts, Raoul studies some stanzas from a poem by DH Lawrence.

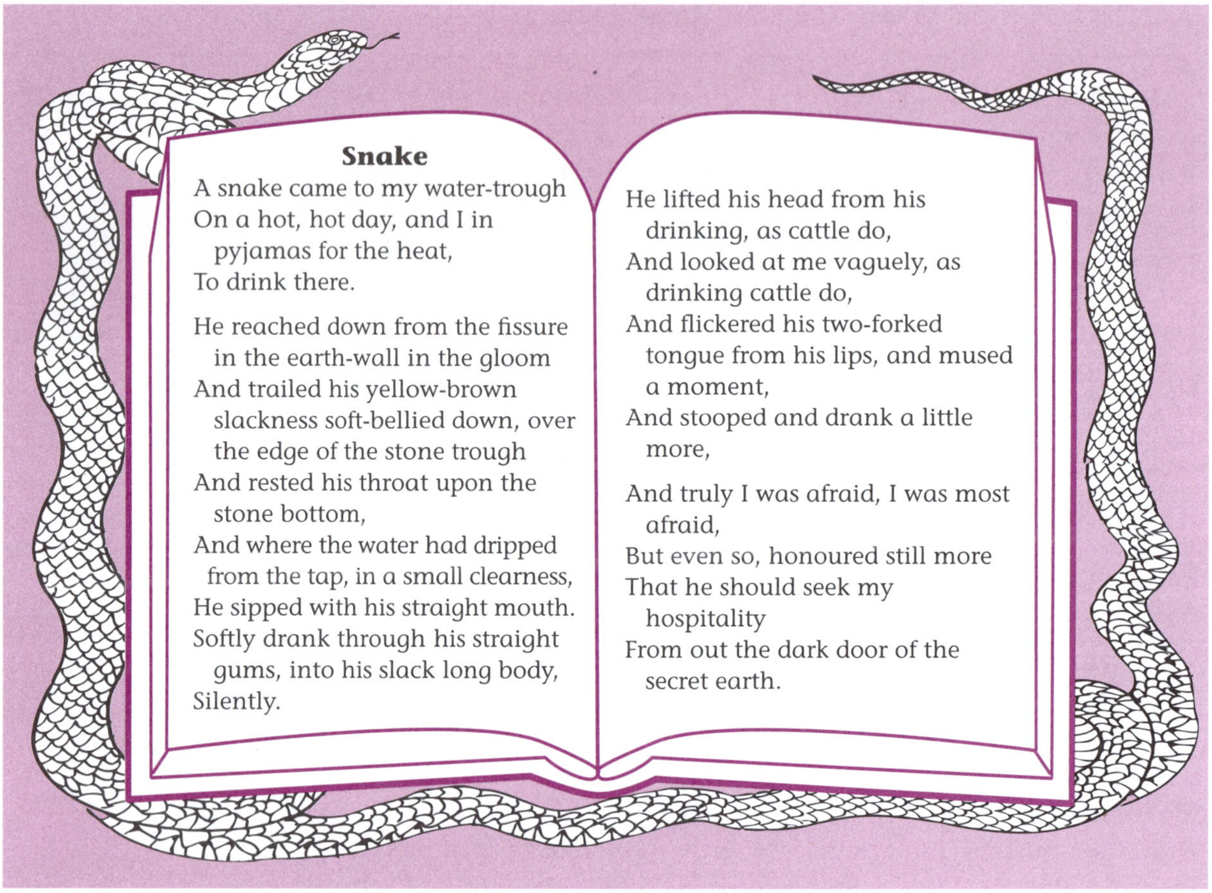

Snake

A snake came to my water-trough
On a hot, hot day, and I in pyjamas for the heat,
To drink there.

He reached down from the fissure in the earth-wall in the gloom
And trailed his yellow-brown slackness soft-bellied down, over the edge of the stone trough
And rested his throat upon the stone bottom,
And where the water had dripped from the tap, in a small clearness,
He sipped with his straight mouth.
Softly drank through his straight gums, into his slack long body,
Silently.

He lifted his head from his drinking, as cattle do,
And looked at me vaguely, as drinking cattle do,
And flickered his two-forked tongue from his lips, and mused a moment,
And stooped and drank a little more,

And truly I was afraid, I was most afraid,
But even so, honoured still more
That he should seek my hospitality
From out the dark door of the secret earth.

1 Which option best describes the poet's feelings about the snake?

- **a** He is angry with it for using his water trough. ☐
- **b** He is both fascinated by it and frightened of it. ☐
- **c** He is both envious and afraid of it. ☐

2 Many words in the second stanza start with the letter *s*. Why do you think the poet has chosen these words? ______________________________

____

3 Which words in the text are similar in meaning to:

- **a** crevice? ____________ **b** looseness? ____________
- **c** absent-mindedly? ____________ **d** fluttered? ____________
- **e** thought? ____________ **f** bent? ____________

Writing the first draft

Raoul remembers the mixed feelings he had about the fish he caught the first time he went deep-sea fishing with his dad. He is going to write about that experience. This is his **first draft**. Read what he wrote, and then answer the questions.

Fish

I held onto the rail as they started the engine.
I was so excited.
I looked at my fishing rod.
It was in its cup, pointing up at the sky.
We sailed quickly out to sea.
Finally they cut the engine.
The boat moved up and down.
I got my fishing rod—
my birthday present—
and took hold of it.
I baited the hook and threw in the line.
I did it well.
I waited a while
But then I felt something pull on the line.
It was a fish.
I was so excited.
When I reeled it in I saw it was a big one.
I was really proud of myself.
But as I watched it moving about on the deck,
I felt sad.
Its scales were shiny and its eyes were huge.
Its fins were so thin and I knew the air would kill it.
Then I saw the hook sticking out of its mouth in a horrible way.
So I bent down and pulled out the hook.
Then I let the fish go.

1 A good **free verse poem** should contain the following features. Tick (✓) the ones that Raoul has used.

- **a** **stanzas** made up of **irregular lines** ☐
- **b** **lines** that consist of **single words**, **phrases** or **sentences** (e.g. *Waited, Felt a pull on the line, Reeled it in, It was a big one*) ☐
- **c** **figurative language**, such as **similes** and **metaphors** (e.g. *as shiny as polished silver*) ☐
- **d** **language** that **shows** rather than tells (e.g. *flailing feebly on the deck* shows helplessness) ☐

2 Raoul writes that the fishing rod was in its cup pointing up at the sky. Which of the following comparisons creates the best mind picture of the scene?

- **a** It was pointing skywards, like a telephone pole. ☐
- **b** It was pointing skywards, like a mast without a sail. ☐
- **c** It was pointing skywards, like a branch without leaves. ☐

Step-by-step improvement plan

Raoul has structured his poem well, but he wants to make it more powerful and interesting. He also wants to make it sound less like a narrative. He is going to do some practice exercises to find ways to do this and needs your help to complete them.

Step 1: Add interest with descriptive words and phrases

Descriptive words and **phrases** help your readers create clearer mind pictures of the people and things you are writing about.

For example: The phrase *stared longingly* creates a clearer mind picture than the single word *looked*, while the single word *mused* is more effective than the phrase *thought about*.

Using descriptive words and phrases makes your writing more powerful and more interesting to read.

1. Read Raoul's draft again and underline the words and phrases listed below. Replace each one with a more **descriptive word** from the box.

Tip! Use a dictionary to help you.

a moved up and down ____________________

b well ____________________

c pull ____________________

d moving about ____________________

e thin ____________________

f sticking out ____________________

g in a horrible way ____________________

tug	properly
flimsy	drag
protruding	monstrously
struggling	flapping
grotesquely	slim
expertly	bulging
rocked	bobbed

2. In the following sentences, circle the most **descriptive** option in each case.

a My fishing rod was (resting, nestling, sitting) in its cup.

b The boat (zoomed, sped, sailed) across the water.

c I (took, grabbed, snatched) my fishing rod.

d I gently (felt, touched, caressed) the handle.

e I (threw, sent, flicked) in the line.

Step 2: Show, don't tell

Show, don't tell is a style of writing that allows your readers to experience the action through their senses. It is the difference between **reporting** something (telling) and **suggesting** something (showing).

For example: *He was very frightened* is telling. *Heart thudding in his chest* is showing.

Using the show, don't tell technique makes your writing more interesting and powerful.

1. Once again, look at Raoul's draft on the previous page. Highlight the phrases, clauses and sentences that could be replaced with the following. Write the new phrase or sentence above or below the original one.
   - **a** The boat cut a foamy trail through the water.
   - **b** Finally a sharp tug!
   - **c** scales sparkling in the sunlight
   - **d** staring eyes
   - **e** gills breathing in the dangerous air
2. Rewrite the following so that you are **showing**, not telling.
   - **a** I was so excited. ______________________________

     ____
   - **b** It looked so weak and helpless. ______________________________

     ____
   - **c** I felt admiration for it. ______________________________

     ____

     ____

Step 3: Add interest with alliteration

Alliteration is the **repetition** of **initial consonant** sounds in words that are close to one another.

For example: *Softly drank through his straight gums, into his slack long body, Silently.*

Alliteration creates a special sound effect that adds rhythm and interest to your writing.

1. Underline the **alliterative** words in the following sentences.
   - **a** The flimsy feather floated onto the fan.
   - **b** The proud peacock showed off its brilliant plumage.
   - **c** The big blue ball bounced down the stairs.
   - **d** The cheeky children chattered well into the night.
   - **e** The runners wore red ribbons on their vests.
2. Find words that start with the letters supplied to complete the following lines.
   - **a** The boat cut a foamy trail through the s______________ water as we s______________ out to s______________
   - **b** boat b______________ gently on the s______________ swell
   - **c** I reached for my f______________ rod and f______________ my f______________ around the handle
   - **d** Fins spread out like f______________ f______________.
   - **e** S______________ I saluted him and returned him to the s______________.

Writing the final draft

This is Raoul's **final draft**. Read the comments about his poem on the left, and do the tasks on the right.

Comments

Using **figures of speech** *like* **similes** *helps the reader create mind pictures of the scene.*

Using **descriptive** *words and phrases adds interest to the poem.*

Showing, *not telling, allows the reader to experience the action through his or her senses.*

Using **alliteration** *adds rhythm and interest to the poem.*

Fish

I held onto the gleaming rail as the engine
roared into life.
Heart racing, fishing rod nestling in its cup
Pointing skywards, like a mast without a sail.
The boat cut a foamy trail through the silver water
as we sped out to sea.
Engine cut
Boat bobbing gently on the soft swell I reached
for my fishing rod,
Folded my fingers around the handle
Carefully– a birthday present.
Baited the hook, flicked in
the line–expertly.
Waited.
Finally a sharp tug.
Heart pounding, I set the hook, played him,
reeled him in.
A big one.
And truly I was proud, I was most proud,
But even so, sad to watch him
flapping furiously on the deck,
Silver scales sparkling in the sunlight,
Staring eyes,
Fins spread out like flimsy fans,
Gills breathing in the dangerous air.
And the hook–the hook protruding grotesquely
From the side of his mouth.
I stooped down and removed it–gently.
Silently I saluted him and returned him to the sea.

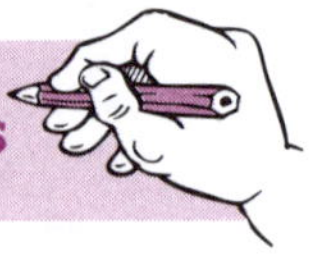

Tasks

1. **Highlight** the **simile**.
2. **Circle** the **verbs** that mean *moved quickly* and *moved up and down*.
3. **Underline** the words that **show** that the writer was **excited**.
4. **Highlight** three examples of **alliteration**.
5. **Underline** the words that **show** that the writer had respect for the fish.

Student B: Suyin's draft

Before writing her first draft, Suyin, another Year 6 student, is going to study some stanzas from the following DH Lawrence poem.

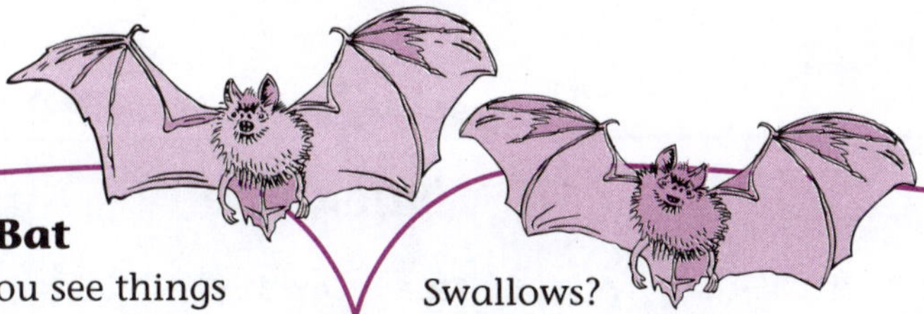

Bat

Look up, and you see things flying
Between the day and the night;
Swallows with spools of dark thread sewing the shadows together.

A circle swoop, and a quick parabola under the bridge arches
Where light pushes through;
A sudden turning upon itself of a thing in the air.
A dip in the water.

And you think:
"The swallows are flying so late!"

Swallows?

Never swallows!
Bats!

Bats, and an uneasy creeping in one's scalp
As the bats swoop overhead!
Flying madly.
Bats!

Creatures that hang themselves up like an old rag, to sleep;
And disgustingly upside down.
Hanging upside down like rows of disgusting old rags
And grinning in their sleep.

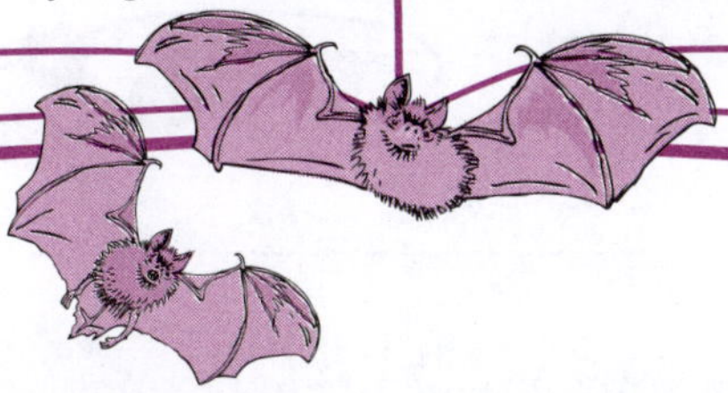

1 How has the poet **personified** the swallows (bats) in the first stanza?

Tip! Remember: personification gives animals and things human qualities.

2 What are the poet's feelings about the bats when he thinks they are swallows?

3 Which two words in the final stanza most strongly express the poet's feelings about the bats?

Writing the first draft

Suyin likes the way the poet expresses the change in his feelings when he realises that the swallows are really bats. She remembers a time when her feelings changed from anger to remorse (feeling sorry for what she had done), and is going to base her poem on that event. This is her **first draft**. Read what she wrote, and then answer the questions.

Necklace

I remember the day my little sister
broke my red necklace.
I found the beads lying all over
the floor.
I was furious!
I called her horrible names and
went to her room.
I stood and looked at her with
my hands on my hips.
She was sitting on the floor
With her face in her hands,
Crying her eyes out.
I felt so bad.
She heard me and looked up.
Her face was red from crying and
there were tears on her cheeks.
She looked so small and scared.
Suddenly I felt awful
that I'd shouted at her,
So I sat down beside her and
Gave her a hug.

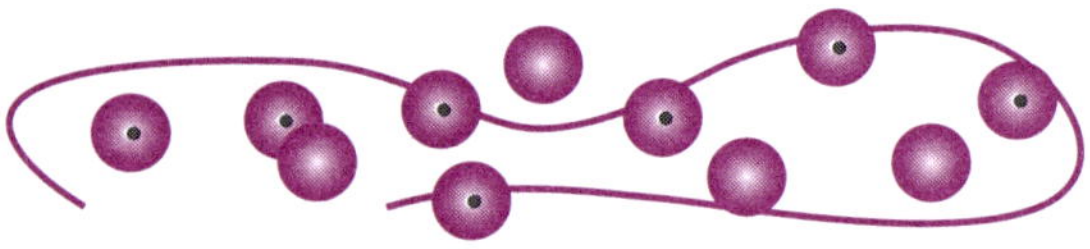

1. Which of these features has Suyin remembered to include in her draft?

   a **stanzas** made up of **irregular lines** ☐

   b **figurative language**, such as **similes** and **metaphors** ☐

   c **language** that **shows** rather than tells ☐

2. Underline the adjective in Suyin's draft that describes extreme anger.

3. Match the following sentences with the **change of feelings** they express.

a The party was a complete disaster, and I had been so looking forward to it.	surprise to acceptance
b I was completely taken aback when I first heard what the plan was, but I gradually got used to the idea.	anxiety to relief
c I thought I was going to miss my plane, but I made it to the airport just in time.	expectation to disappointment

Step-by-step improvement plan

Like Raoul, Suyin wants to express the change in her feelings in a more powerful and interesting way. Complete these practice exercises to help her finds ways to do this.

Step 1: Add interest with descriptive words and phrases

1. In the following sentences, replace the underlined word or phrase with a more **descriptive** one from the box.

concealed	marched	supported	stretched	scattered
buried	proceeded	sobbing	cradled	whining

a Beads were spilt ______________ across the floor.

b I went ______________ into her room.

c She was sitting on the floor, crying ______________ .

d Her face was hidden ______________ in her little hands.

e I held ______________ her in my arms.

2. Use the following words to write interesting **descriptions** that Suyin could use in her poem. The descriptions do not have to be full sentences.

Tip! Look up the meanings of any words you are unsure of.

a livid ______________________________

____

b raged ______________________________

____

c puckered ______________________________

____

d cowering ______________________________

____

e trembled ______________________________

____

Step 2: Show, don't tell

Tip! Remember—**showing** suggests and **telling** reports. When writing **poems** and **narratives**, showing is usually more effective than telling.

1. Do the following phrases and sentences **show** or **tell**? Write *S* or *T* in the boxes.

a I was furious. ☐

b My blood was boiling. ☐

c She was terrified. ☐

d She was shaking like a leaf. ☐

e My heart lurched. ☐

f I felt awful. ☐

g It was a cold morning. ☐

h The morning air was bitter. ☐

i His stomach is growling. ☐

j He is hungry. ☐

2 Rewrite the following sentences so that they tell what the girl is feeling.

Example: She poured her heart out. She expressed her feelings freely.

a She wished the earth would swallow her up. ____________________

b Steam was coming out her ears. ____________________

c Her heart was breaking. ____________________

d She was cowering in the corner. ____________________

Step 3: Add interest with similes

Remember—a **simile** is a **figure of speech** that **compares** two unlike things using the words *like* or *as*.

For example: *Red beads lay everywhere,* **like** *tiny drops of blood.*

Tiny beads **as** *red* **as** *blood lay everywhere.*

Similes add **interest** and **energy** to our writing.

1 We often use **similes** to express our **emotions**; for example, *Fear swept over her* **like** *an icy wind.*

Complete each of the similes below with one of these comparisons.

- a poisonous liquid
- mice gnawing on a rope
- a startled rabbit
- ice touched by the sun's warmth
- a bird trapped in a cage
- a volcano about to erupt

a My heart fluttered inside my chest, like ____________________

b My heart jumped, like ____________________

c Jealousy seeped through her heart, like ____________________

d Anger bubbled inside her, like ____________________

e Anxiety tugged at her heart, like ____________________

f My heart melted, like ____________________

2 Look at the first two **similes** in the exercise above (**a** and **b**). Which emotions might they be describing?

a ____________________ **b** ____________________

3 Similes are also effective in describing the way things look. Complete each of the following **similes** with a suitable comparison.

a I stood before her, hands on hips, arms jutting out like ____________________.

b Her little hands were as soft and delicate as ____________________.

c She looked at me, her eyes as dark as ____________________.

Writing the final draft

Suyin has started writing the **final draft** of her **poem**. Help her complete it and then look in the answers section to compare what you have written with what Suyin wrote.

Hint! Look at Suyin's first draft and practice exercises for ideas.

Necklace

My little sister broke my red necklace
Beads scattered across the floor
like **(Complete the simile.)**____________________
my blood b____________ **(Complete the word.)**
I called her names
I r____________ madly.
I m____________ into her room
Hands on hips, arms
Jutting out like **(Complete the simile.)**____________________
She was sitting on the floor—crying, s____________
(Where was her face?)

____

hands as soft and delicate as **(Complete the simile.)** ____________
She heard me and looked up
(What did her face look like?)

____

Tear-stained cheeks
Eyes filled with f____________.
My heart l____________,
Hard cold heart
Melted,
Like **(Complete the simile.)** ____________________

____

I sat down beside her and
c____________ her in my arms

Your turn

Write a **free verse poem** on one of the following. Use your own paper for this activity.

Writing Checklist Make sure you: ✓

- divide your poem into **stanzas**. ☐
- use some **descriptive** or **figurative language**, such as **alliteration** and **similes**. ☐
- use the **show, don't tell** technique. ☐

Tip Use **Raoul's final draft** on page 78 and Suyin's **final draft** on page 83 to help you write your poem.

Go to WORD BANK page 122 for useful vocabulary

1. Write about a time when you experienced mixed feelings about something. Use Raoul's poem as a model.
2. Write about a time when something happened that caused a sudden change in your feelings. Use Suyin's poem as a model.
3. Write your own animal poem based on DH Lawrence's poems 'Snake' and 'Bat'. How did you feel as you watched the animal?
4. Write a free verse poem about an oak tree. Use the information below to help you.

Oaks are sturdy trees with thick trunks and spreading branches. They make excellent shade trees. Some are 200 years old and more. Their wood is strong and hard and is used to make furniture and floorboards. On average, they reach a height of 16–23 m.

They have broad leaves that grow in spirals and bear a nut-like fruit called an acorn. In autumn their leaves turn brown, yellow and red before drifting to the ground. They come to life again in spring, when vibrant green leaves and flowers start to appear.

Unit 8 Biographies

Looking at biographies

A **biography** is the story of a real person's life, written by someone else. If someone writes his or her own life story, it is called an **autobiography**. Biographies and autobiographies are both a type of **recount**.

Like all recounts, a **biography** should have:

- an **introduction** that answers the questions **who**, **what**, **where** and **when**.
- **paragraphs** that give a **chronological** account of **events** in the person's life.
- a **conclusion** that wraps up the biography with a **comment** on the contribution the person has made, or that **summarises** or **evaluates** the person's achievements.

1 The text below is the first paragraph of an **autobiography**. Rewrite it so that you are the one telling the story of Arun's life. Start by replacing the first word with *Arun*, and then change the pronouns from the first person (*I, me, my*) to the third person (*he, him, his*).

> I was born in a small country town on 1 January 2000. My parents named me Arun because it means 'dawn' in Hindi. They chose this name for several reasons: I was their first child; they had only recently arrived in Australia from India; and I had come into the world on the first day of the new millennium. My name therefore symbolised a number of new beginnings for them.

2 Use the information in the box to write the first paragraph of a **biography** of Bill Gates, the co-founder of Microsoft.

> **Full name**: William Henry Gates
> **Date of birth**: 28 October 1955
> **Place of birth**: Seattle, USA
> **Family information**: son of William and Mary Gates—one of three children—has an older and younger sister

Student A: Bella's draft

The students in Bella's Year 6 history class have been learning about Australia's development as a nation. They have compiled a list of people from Australia's past who made a valuable contribution to Australia and, in some cases, to the rest of the world as well.

Caroline Chisholm (humanitarian—helped female immigrants)
Edward Hargraves (discovered gold 1851)
Dame Nellie Melba (opera singer)
Sir Charles Kingsford Smith (aviator)
John Flynn (started the Flying Doctor Service)
Edith Cowan (helped set up the Children's Protection Society)
Eddie Mabo (campaigned for Indigenous land rights)
Elizabeth Macarthur (pioneer—wool industry in Australia)
Howard Florey (role in the development of penicillin)
Andrew 'Banjo' Paterson (poet)

The students now have to write a **biography** of one of the people on the list.

Bella is going to write about Elizabeth Macarthur. She starts by jotting down what she knows about her life.

Born: 14 August 1766, Devon (England)
Husband: John Macarthur, army officer
Why she came to Australia: Husband part of New South Wales Corps
Date of arrival: 28 June 1790 (on the Scarborough, part of the Second Fleet)
Children: Gave birth to 9 children—7 survived childhood
Important life events:
- husband granted land near Parramatta—Elizabeth farm—later granted more land south of Sydney—Camden park—bred merino sheep—sent first bale of wool to England 1807
- 1808 husband quarrelled with governor (William Bligh)—had to return to England—gone for 9 years—Elizabeth looked after family, farms and sheep—helped build up flocks—helped make New south Wales an important centre for wool production

Died: 9 February 1850, New South Wales

1. How would the establishment of the wool trade have helped the colony of New South Wales? ____________________

2. How did the discovery of gold in 1851 change Australia's population?

Writing the first draft

This is Bella's **first draft**. Read what she wrote, and then answer the questions.

Elizabeth Macarthur

Elizabeth Macarthur was born in Devon, England. She was born on 14 August 1766. She helped start the wool trade in Australia.

Elizabeth came to Australia with her husband. That was in 1790. Her husband's name was John. He was an army officer. He was given 100 acres of land near Parramatta, where he was commandant. He called the property Elizabeth farm and built a house. Elizabeth said it was "a very excellent brick building". He was given more land and called it Camden park.

John bought some merino sheep. They produced good wool. Elizabeth helped him build up their flocks. They started exporting wool to England.

John often quarrelled with people. The governor of New south Wales was William Bligh. John quarrelled with him and had to go back to England. He was away for nine years. Elizabeth was left to look after their seven children, their farms and their sheep. She did a great job. John wrote her letters telling her what to do. She did everything he said. John came back to Australia in 1817.

1. A good **biography** should contain the following features. Tick (✓) the ones that Bella has used in her draft.

   a an **opening paragraph** that gives the reader some **background information** on the person and briefly answers the questions **who**, **what, where** and **when** ☐

   b **paragraphs** that give an account of **events** in the person's life, usually in chronological order ☐

   c mainly **past-tense verbs** (e.g. *came, bought*) ☐

   d **pronouns in the third person** (e.g. *she, they*) ☐

   e **time connectives** that link events (e.g. *then, after a few years*) ☐

   f **evaluative language** (e.g. *excellent, great*) ☐

   g **correct spelling** and **punctuation** ☐

   h a **conclusion** that **wraps up** the biography with a **comment** on the contribution the person has made ☐

2. Combine the following sets of sentences into a **single sentence**.

   a Elizabeth Macarthur was born in Devon, England. She was born on 14 August 1766.

   ____

   ____

   b Elizabeth came to Australia with her husband. That was in 1790. Her husband's name was John. ______________________________

   ____

   ____

Step-by-step improvement plan

Bella has done a number of things well in her draft, but she can improve on it. She is going to do some practice exercises to find ways to do this. Help her complete them.

Step 1: Use time connectives to link events

Time connectives are words and phrases that show the **sequence** of **events**.
For example: *First, After that.*
Using time connectives to link events makes your writing flow.

Bella has used some dates in her biography, but she hasn't used them to link events. Help her **link** the **events** in the following paragraphs with the words, phrases and clauses from the box.

by the time John returned	shortly afterwards	today
after arguing with the governor	soon	during that time

John and Elizabeth Macarthur arrived in Sydney in June 1790. ____________________ John was granted 100 acres of land in Parramatta. He called the property Elizabeth Farm. ____________ Elizabeth Farm is a museum.

John Macarthur bought his first merino sheep in 1796. He and Elizabeth worked hard to build up their flocks and ______________ they had 4000 almost-pure merinos.

John was an argumentative man. ______________________________, he was forced to return to England. He stayed there for nine years. ______________________________ Elizabeth managed the flocks, with great success.

____, the wool industry in New South Wales was well established.

Step 2: Use capital letters for proper nouns

A **noun** names a person, place or thing. **Common nouns** name general people, places and things, while **proper nouns** name specific people, places and things.

Using capital letters for proper nouns shows that they are unique.

For example: The word *farm* is written with a small letter when it refers to a farm in general, but when it is part of the name of a specific farm, it is written with a capital letter; e.g. *Redhill Farm.*

When a proper noun contains more than one word, all of the words usually start with a capital letter; e.g. *Great Britain.* However, **prepositions** and other little words that come in the middle of a proper noun have small (lower-case) letters.

For example: *The Department* **of** *Agriculture* **and** *Water Resources.*

Tip! The titles of books, poems, songs, films and television programs are all **proper nouns**.

1 Rewrite the following proper nouns with the correct punctuation.

western australia ______________________________

the man from snowy river ______________________________

caroline chisholm college ______________________________

mother teresa primary school ______________________________

national gallery of australia ______________________________

queen victoria museum and art gallery ______________________________

university of the sunshine coast ______________________________

2 In her notes and draft Bella has written three proper nouns with small letters. Go through her notes and draft again and make the corrections for her.

Step 3: Use evaluative language to express opinions and judgements

Evaluative language is language that expresses feelings, opinions, judgements and points of view. It can be **positive** or **negative**.

For example: *The Macarthurs were* **successful** *sheep farmers.* (positive evaluation)
John Macarthur often **argued** *with people in authority.* (negative evaluation)

We can use adjectives, verbs, adverbs, adverbial phrases and adjectival phrases to evaluate people and things.

For example: *He was often* **in a bad mood**. (adjectival phrase)

Using **evaluative language** in a **biography** helps you paint a picture of the person's **strengths** and **weaknesses**.

1 State whether the underlined words or phrases in the following sentences express a **positive** or a **negative evaluation**.

- **a** Elizabeth Macarthur wrote that their home at Elizabeth Farm was "a very excellent brick building". ______________
- **b** In those early years, life in the colony could be extremely harsh. ______________
- **c** Elizabeth Macarthur was a well-educated woman. ______________
- **d** John Macarthur was granted two large properties in Parramatta and south of Sydney. ______________
- **e** Many of the other farmers cross-bred their merino sheep with other breeds, resulting in poorer quality wool. ______________

2 Use the phrases in brackets to help you write interesting **sentences** about Elizabeth Macarthur.

- **a** (helped her husband) ______________________________
____
- **b** (an important role) ______________________________
____

Writing the final draft

This is Bella's **final draft** of her **biography**. Read the comments about her biography on the left, and do the tasks on the right.

Comments

The **opening paragraph** *tells* **who, what, when** *and* ***where***.

Using **time connectives** *helps to link events and makes the writing flow.*

Using **evaluative language** *helps the writer paint a picture of people's strengths and weaknesses.*

A good **conclusion** *wraps up the biography and includes a* **comment** *on the contribution the person has made.*

Elizabeth Macarthur

Elizabeth Macarthur was born in Devon, England on 14 August 1766. She came to Australia with her husband, John, an army officer, in June 1790. She is best known for her role in starting the wool industry in Australia.

Shortly after arriving in New South Wales, John Macarthur was granted 100 acres of land in Parramatta, where he held the position of commandant. He named the property Elizabeth Farm, in honour of his wife. In letters to her family in England, Elizabeth described her house as "a very excellent brick building". Today Elizabeth Farm is a museum. In 1805 John Macarthur was granted another large property south of Sydney, which he named Camden Park.

In 1796 John Macarthur bought his first merino sheep, a breed that produces very good wool. Other farmers in the area also bought merino sheep, but they cross-bred them with other breeds, which affected the quality of the wool. John and Elizabeth worked hard to build up their flock, and by 1803 they had 4000 almost-pure merinos. They sent their first bale of wool to England in 1807.

John Macarthur was an argumentative man who often clashed with people in authority. In 1808 he quarrelled with the governor of New South Wales, William Bligh, and was forced to leave the colony for nine years. During that time Elizabeth not only took care of their seven surviving children and household affairs, but she also looked after the flocks at both Elizabeth Farm and Camden Park—with great success. She wrote long letters to her husband in England, giving him detailed reports, and followed the instructions in his letters for further developing their flocks.

By the time Elizabeth's husband returned to Australia in 1817, New South Wales had become known in Britain and other countries as a centre for wool production. John Macarthur is usually referred to as the founder of the wool industry in Australia. However, he could not have achieved his success without Elizabeth's help and support.

Tasks

1. **Circle** the **proper nouns**.
2. **Highlight** three **time connectives**.
3. **Underline** the phrase that expresses a **positive evaluation** of merino wool.
4. **Highlight** three separate words that help paint a **negative** image of John Macarthur.
5. **Underline** the sentence that **highlights** Elizabeth Macarthur's role in establishing the wool industry in Australia.

Student B: Harrison's draft

Harrison, another Year 6 student, is going to write about Charles Kingsford Smith. He also starts by jotting down what he knows about Charles Kingsford Smith's life.

Born: 9 February 1897, Brisbane (Queensland)
Family: 7th child of William Smith (banker) and Mary Kingsford
Early life: spent 4 years in Canada—returned to Sydney 1907—went to St Andrew's cathedral school and Sydney technical high school
First World War: fought at Gallipoli and in Egypt and France—started training as a pilot in 1916—awarded Military cross for bravery
After the war: worked as a stunt flier in circus (USA)—worked for a joy-riding company in Sydney—pilot for Western Australian airways—started interstate flying services with 2 partners
Important achievements: flew right around Australia (10 days, 5 hrs); from California to Brisbane (83 hrs 38 mins) in the Southern cross; Ireland to Newfoundland ($31\frac{1}{2}$ hours); solo from England to Darwin (just under 10 days—record); knighted (became Sir Charles Kingsford Smith) in 1932
Died: 6 November 1935—plane crashed into sea on way from England to Australia
Tributes: Sydney airport named after him—once featured on Australian $20 note

1. Look carefully at the pictures and then answer the questions.
   Why do you think pilots of early aeroplanes had to wear goggles and leather helmets such as the ones shown in the picture? ______________________

2. Based on the information in Harrison's notes, which of the following adjectives could be used to describe Charles Kingsford Smith?

- adventurous ☐
- cowardly ☐
- courageous ☐
- hesitant ☐
- timid ☐
- determined ☐

Writing the first draft

This is Harrison's **first draft**. Read what he wrote and then answer the questions.

Charles Kingsford Smith

Charles Kingsford Smith was born on 9 February 1897. He was born in Brisbane. His father's name was William Smith and he was a banker. His mother's name was Mary Kingsford. He was their seventh child.

His family spent four years in Canada. They came back to Australia and he went to school in Sydney.

He fought in the First World War. He fought at Gallipoli and in Egypt and France. That's when he started training as a pilot. He got the Military cross for bravery.

He flew stunt planes and took people for joy rides. He started his own company called Interstate flying services. He and his partners needed money, so they did some demonstration flights. They flew right around Australia. It took them just over ten days. They flew from California to Brisbane in the Southern cross. It took them more than 83 hours. He also made other important flights, like flying from England to Darwin in record-breaking time.

He was knighted in 1932 and died in 1935 when his plane crashed into the sea.

1 A good **biography** should contain the following features. Tick (✓) the ones that Harrison has used in his draft.

- **a** an **opening paragraph** that gives the reader some **background information** on the person and briefly answers the questions **who**, **what, where**, **when** or **why** ☐
- **b** **paragraphs** that give an account of **events** in the person's life, usually in chronological order ☐
- **c** mainly **past-tense verbs** ☐
- **d** **pronouns** in the **third person** ☐
- **e** **time connectives** that link events ☐
- **f** **evaluative language** ☐
- **g** **correct spelling** and **punctuation** ☐
- **h** a **conclusion** that **wraps up** the biography with a **comment** on the contribution the person has made to society ☐

2 Look at Harrison's introduction to help you fill in the missing information in the following paragraph.

Charles Kingsford Smith was born in ________________ on 9 February 1897. He was the ________________________ of ____________________, a banker, and __________ ________________.

3 Suggest two ways in which flying today is different from flying in the 1920s and 1930s.

____

____

____

Step-by-step improvement plan

Harrison has also done some things well in his draft, but like Bella, he is going to do some practice exercises to find ways to improve it. Help him complete the exercises.

Step 1: Use time connectives to link events

Complete the following paragraphs with the words, phrases and clauses in the box. Use each **time connective** once.

after	when they returned to Australia		first
when he was a child	then	during the First World War	after the war

________________, Charles Kingsford Smith's family spent four years in Canada.

________________________, Charles completed his education in Sydney.

____________________, Charles fought at Gallipoli and in Egypt and France. He started training as a pilot and was made a lieutenant __________ being awarded the Military Cross for bravery.

________________ Charles continued to fly planes. __________ he worked as a stunt flier in a circus in the United States, and __________ he joined a joy-riding company in Sydney.

Step 2: Use capital letters for proper nouns

Harrison has written the following **proper nouns** incorrectly in his notes and draft. Help him correct them.

Southern cross ____________________

Sydney airport ____________________

St Andrew's cathedral school ____________________

Sydney technical high school ____________________

Interstate flying services ____________________

Step 3: Pack more information into sentences

In Unit 1 you learnt that a **sentence** is a group of words that makes complete sense and that packing information from two or three sentences into one sentence makes your writing tighter and easier to read.

For example: *Charles Kingsford Smith was born in 1897. He was a pioneer of aviation.*
Charles Kingsford Smith, a pioneer of aviation, was born in 1897.

1. Write the following sets of sentences as a **single sentence**. Use the clues in brackets to help you.

   a In 1916 he started training as a pilot. He was appointed a flying officer the following year. (Use the conjunction *and.*)

   ____

   ____

b Charles formed his own flying company. It was called Interstate Flying Services. He formed it with two other pilots. (Use commas and leave out *He formed it*.)

c In 1930 Charles launched Australian National Airways. He completed a crossing from Ireland to Newfoundland. It took him 31½ hours. (Use the conjunction *and* and replace *It took him* with *in*.)

2 Now try the following on your own.

a Later that year Charles flew from England to Darwin. He flew solo. He did it in a record-breaking time. He did it in less than ten days.

b On 6 November 1935 Charles and another pilot took off from England. They wanted to try for another record-breaking flight to Australia. Their plane crashed into the sea. Both pilots were lost.

Step 4: Wrap up your biography with a good conclusion

Harrison's **biography** needs one more paragraph in which he comments in some way on Charles Kingsford Smith's contribution to Australian life.

He could include the following information in his conclusion:

Australia has recognised his contribution to aviation.	Sydney airport is named after him.	He was once featured on the $20 note.

Now use the information to write a good **concluding paragraph**.

Writing the final draft

Harrison has started writing the **final draft** of Charles Kingsford Smith's **biography**. Help him complete it and then look in the answers section to compare what you have written with what Harrison wrote.

Hint! Look at Harrison's first draft and practice exercises for ideas.

Sir Charles Kingsford Smith

Charles Kingsford Smith, a pioneer of aviation in Australia, was born on 9 February 1897 in Brisbane. He was the seventh child of William Smith, a banker, and Mary Kingsford. His family spent four years in Canada when he was a child, but they returned to Sydney in 1907. Charles completed his education in Sydney at St Andrew's Cathedral School and later at Sydney Technical High School. **(Write about Charles Kingsford Smith's part in the First World War.)**

....

....

....

....

....

....

Charles continued to fly planes after the war. First he worked as a stunt flier in a circus in the United States, and then he joined a joy-riding company in Sydney. He also worked as a pilot for Western Australian Airways for a while. However, he wanted to start his own flying company, and, together with two other pilots, formed Interstate Flying Services. In order to raise money, Charles and one of his partners completed some important demonstration flights. **(Continue the paragraph by writing about their flights around Australia and from California to Brisbane.)**

....

....

....

....

In 1930 Charles launched Australian National Airways and completed a trans-Atlantic crossing from Ireland to Newfoundland in $31\frac{1}{2}$ hours. Later that year he flew solo from England to Darwin in a record-breaking time of just less than 10 days. He was knighted for his services to aviation in 1932. **(Write about Charles Kingsford Smith's final flight in 1935.)**

....

....

(Write the conclusion.) ....

....

....

....

Your turn

Write a **biography** of one to two pages on one of the following people. Use your own paper for this activity.

Writing Checklist Make sure your biography includes: ✓

- an **opening paragraph** that gives the reader some **background information** on the person and briefly answers the questions **who, what, where, when** or **why**. ☐
- **paragraphs** that give a chronological account of **events** in the person's life. ☐
- mainly **past-tense verbs**. ☐
- **pronouns** in the **third person**. ☐
- **time connectives** that link events. ☐
- **evaluative language**. ☐
- **well-constructed sentences**. ☐
- **correct spelling** and **punctuation**. ☐
- a **conclusion** that **wraps up** the biography with a comment on the contribution the person has made to society, or that **summarises** or **evaluates** the person's achievements. ☐

Tip Use **Bella's final draft** on page 90 and **Harrison's final draft** on page 95 to help you.

Go to WORD BANK page 122 for useful vocabulary

1. Research the life of one of the other people on the list that Harrison and Bella's Year 6 class drew up and then write his or her biography.
2. Research the life of someone you admire and then write his or her biography.
3. Research the life of one of the following famous Australians and then write his or her biography:

David Gulpilil
(actor)

Anh Do
(comedian)

Evonne Goolagong Cawley
(tennis player)

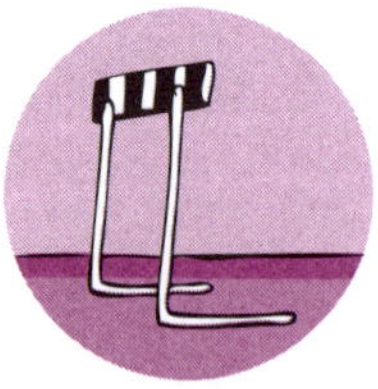

Sally Pearson
(athlete)

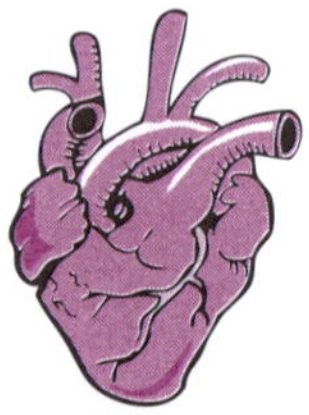

Victor Chang
(heart surgeon)

Unit 9 Compare and contrast texts

Looking at texts that compare and contrast

Texts that **compare** and **contrast** look at the **similarities** and **differences** between people, places, things or situations. Comparing and contrasting information forms a part of texts such as discussions and debates. However, it can also be a text on its own.

A text that **compares** and **contrasts** should have:

- an **opening paragraph** that briefly states **who** or **what** is being **compared/contrasted**.
- **middle paragraphs** that show **how** the people or things being compared/contrasted are **alike** and **different**.
- a **conclusion** that **sums up** the information in the text by looking at both the similarities and differences between the people or things being compared/contrasted.

1. Look at the list of **similarities** and **differences** between houses and nests.

Similarities	Differences
both offer shelter	nests are for animals, houses are for humans
both have to be built	nests are usually built in trees, houses on the ground

Use the above information to complete the following paragraph.

While there are ____________________ between nests and houses, there are also ____________________. They are similar because ______________________________

____

____

The main reason they are different is that ______________________________

____

____

2. Write down three **similarities** and three **differences** between dogs and cats.

Similarities: ______________________________

____

Differences: ______________________________

____

Student A: Josh's draft

The students in Josh's Year 6 class have been researching the way of life of children around the world. Now they have to use the information they have collected to **compare** and **contrast** the lives of two imaginary children from two different countries.

Josh is going to compare the lives of Shunyuan, a Chinese boy who lives in China's capital, Beijing, and Owen, a British boy who lives in Windsor, a town in Berkshire, England.

These are the notes Josh has made about each boy.

Shunyuan

- 11 years old—final year primary school—lives in Beijing, China—speaks Mandarin

School:

- starts at 7:30am, ends at 5 pm
- subjects—e.g. Chinese (Mandarin), English (second language) maths, science, history, geography, art—PE—group exercises every day combined with flag-raising ceremony and singing of national anthem
- gets lots of homework—often goes to bed at 11 pm

Home and family:

- lives in 2-bedroom apartment in high rise
- lives with mother and father
- an only child
- no pets

Leisure activities:

- very little time for leisure activities—sometimes plays soccer, basketball, table tennis, computer games

Future goals:

- wants to work with animals one day

Owen

- 11 years old—final year primary school—lives in Windsor in Berkshire, England—speaks English

School:

- starts at 8:45 am, ends at 3:30 pm
- subjects—e.g. English, maths, science, history, geography, art, French (second language)—PE—twice a week—does exercises and plays games like soccer and cricket
- homework—about an hour a day

Home and family:

- lives in 3-bedroom house—double storey—big back garden
- lives with mother, father, younger brother and sister
- the family has a dog called Brutus and a cat called Orlando

Leisure activities:

- watches TV - plays computer games—soccer—cricket

Future goals:

- wants to be a vet

Help Josh sort out the similarities and differences between the boys' lives by completing the following table.

Differences: Shunyuan	Similarities	Differences: Owen

Writing the first draft

This is Josh's **first draft**. Read what he has written and then answer the questions.

Shunyuan and Owen

Shunyuan lives in Beijing in China. Owen lives in Windsor in Berkshire, England. The boys are 11 years old. They are in their final year of primary school.

Shunyuan and Owen learn maths, science, geography and history at school. Shunyuan's main language is Mandarin. Owen's is English. Shunyuan can speak a bit of English but Owen can't speak Mandarin. Shunyuan has PE every day. The students do group exercises. Owen has PE twice a week. They do exercises and play games.

Shunyuan is at school from 7:30 am to 5 pm. He gets so much homework that he often goes to bed at 11 pm. He doesn't have much time for leisure activities. Owen only spends about an hour on his homework. Owen has lots of time for leisure activities.

Shunyuan lives with his mum and dad in a two-bedroom apartment in a high-rise building. Owen lives with his mum, dad, brother, sister and two pets in a three-bedroom house. It has two storeys and a big back garden.

Shunyuan wants to work with animals when he grows up. Owen wants to be a vet.

1 A text that **compares** and **contrasts** should contain the following features. Tick (✓) the ones that Josh has used in his draft.

- **a** an **opening paragraph** that briefly states **who** or **what** is being **compared/contrasted** ☐
- **b** **middle paragraphs** that show **how** the subjects are **alike** or **different** ☐
- **c** mainly **present-tense verbs** (e.g. *lives, do*) ☐
- **d** **words** and **phrases** that express **comparison** and **contrast** (e.g. *similarly, on the other hand*) ☐
- **e** **correct spelling** and **punctuation** ☐
- **f** a **conclusion** that **sums up** the information in the text by looking at both the **similarities** and **differences** between the subjects being compared/contrasted ☐

2 Complete the following paragraph by telling how your situation is similar to or different from Shunyuan's and Owen's.

Shunyuan lives in a small apartment with his mother and father, while Owen lives in a three-bedroom, double-storey house with his mother, father, brother, sister and two pets.

My home is similar to/different from ______________________________

____

____

____

____

____

Step-by-step improvement plan

In his draft, Josh has identified the similarities and differences between Shunyuan and Owen's lives. However, he needs to make his writing read more fluently and is going to do some practice exercises to find ways to do this. Help him complete the exercises.

Step 1: Use connectives that show similarity and difference

Connectives are words and phrases that **link ideas**.

For example: *Shunyuan lives in Beijing, the capital city of China. Owen,* ***on the other hand****, lives in a town in Berkshire, England.*

Using connectives to link ideas makes your writing flow better.

Connectives that compare and contrast information can be **conjunctions**.

For example: *although, both ... and, but, even though, unless, whereas, while* and *yet.*

1 Complete each of the following sentences with a **conjunction** from the list. Use a different conjunction each time.

a Shunyuan doesn't have a pet, ________________ he loves animals.

b ________________ the boys come from different backgrounds, their lives are similar in some ways.

c Shunyuan is an only child ________________ Owen has a younger brother and sister.

d ______________ both boys get homework, Shunyuan's load is much greater than Owen's.

e Shunyuan has PE every day, ________________ Owen has it only twice a week.

Connectives that compare and contrast information can also be **adverbs**.

For example: *also, however, too.*

2 Complete the following paragraph with **adverbs** from the list.

The students at Shunyuan's school do group exercises every day. The students at Owen's school do exercises during PE; ________________, they ________________ play games like soccer and cricket.

Connectives that compare and contrast information can also be **prepositional phrases**.

For example: *in contrast, in comparison to, on the other hand.*

3 Fill in the gaps in the following sentences with a **prepositional phrase** from the list. Use a different phrase each time.

a Shunyuan lives in a two-bedroom apartment in a high-rise building. Owen, __________ ______________________, lives in a three-bedroom, double-storey house.

b Shunyuan spends almost ten hours a day at school. Owen, ________________, spends less than seven hours a day at school.

c _______________________________ Shunyuan's work load, Owen's is very light.

Step 2: Use commas to separate words, phrases and clauses

A **comma (,)** is a **punctuation mark** that separates words, phrases and clauses in a sentence. It indicates a slight pause in the sentence.

For example: *The people who live in the house are Owen, his mother, father, brother and sister.*
On the other hand, Shunyuan spends almost ten hours a day at school.
Shunyuan, who comes from China, is in his final year at primary school.
Although Owen gets homework every day, he also has plenty of leisure time.

Using commas in a sentence makes the meaning clear and the sentence easier to read.

Tip! If you are not sure where the pause comes in a sentence, read it out loud.

1 Underline two lists in Josh's draft. Has he used **commas** correctly? ____________

2 Fill in the missing **commas** in the following sentences. Listen for the pauses when you read the sentences out loud.

- **a** Both Shunyuan and Owen live with their parents but whereas Shunyuan is an only child Owen has a younger brother and sister.
- **b** Both boys learn maths science history geography and art but while Owen's main language is English Shunyuan's is Mandarin.

3 Answer the following questions using a **single, full sentence** in each case. Make sure you use **commas** correctly.

Tip! Use Josh's notes and draft to help you answer the questions.

- **a** What does Owen do in his leisure time? ______________________________

  ____

- **b** What are three subjects that both boys study at school, and which subject does Shunyuan study that Owen doesn't study?

  ____

  ____

Step 3: Wrap up your comparison with a good conclusion

In Unit 8 you learnt that the **conclusion** is the final paragraph of a text. It should **wrap up** the text in some way.

In a text that **compares** and **contrasts**, the conclusion should sum up the information by looking at both the **similarities** and **differences** between the people or things being written about.

Which of the following texts best sums up the comparison between Shunyuan and Owen?

- **a** Shunyuan and Owen come from different parts of the world, so their lives are obviously different in many ways. However, as the text shows, there are some similarities in their lives. ☐
- **b** Shunyuan lives in China and Owen lives in England. The two countries have completely different traditions. That's why the boys' lives are so different. ☐

Writing the final draft

This is Josh's **final draft**. Read the comments about his text on the left, and do the tasks on the right.

Comments

*The **opening paragraph** briefly states who or what is being compared and contrasted.*

*Using **connectives** that compare and contrast information helps to link events and makes the writing flow.*

*Using **commas** to separate words, phrases and clauses in sentences makes the meaning clearer and the sentences easier to read.*

*A good **conclusion** wraps up the text by looking at both the similarities and differences between the people or things being written about.*

Shunyuan and Owen

Shunyuan and Owen are 11-year-old boys in their final year in primary school. Shunyuan lives in Beijing, China and Owen lives in Windsor, a town in Berkshire, England. Although the boys come from different backgrounds, their lives are similar in some ways.

One of these similarities is in the subjects they study at school. Both boys learn maths, science, history, geography and art, but while Owen's main language is English, Shunyuan's is Mandarin. Shunyuan can communicate in English, as he studies it as a second language at school, but Owen doesn't know any Mandarin. Owen's second language at school is French.

Another subject both boys do at school is PE. At Shunyuan's school the students do group exercises every day and afterwards they have a flag-raising ceremony and sing the national anthem. Owen has PE twice a week. The students at his school do exercises during PE, but they also play games like cricket and soccer.

One of the big differences between Shunyuan's life and Owen's life is in the number of hours they spend on their schoolwork. Shunyuan's school day begins at 7:30 am and ends at 5 pm. He gets a lot of homework and often goes to bed after 11 pm. Owen's school day starts at 8:45 am and ends at 3:30 pm. Unlike Shunyuan, he doesn't get much homework, so he has plenty of time to do other things, like watch TV and play computer games.

Both Shunyuan and Owen live with their parents, but whereas Shunyuan is an only child, Owen has a younger brother and sister. Owen also has two pets: a dog called Brutus and a cat called Orlando. His family lives in a double-storey house that has three bedrooms and a large back garden. Shunyuan, on the other hand, lives in a two-bedroom apartment in a high-rise building. He does not have a pet, but he loves animals and wants to work with them when he grows up. Owen plans to become a vet, so the boys share an interest in animals.

After looking at both boys' lives, it is clear that even though they live thousands of kilometres apart and come from very different backgrounds, there are some similarities in their lives.

Tasks

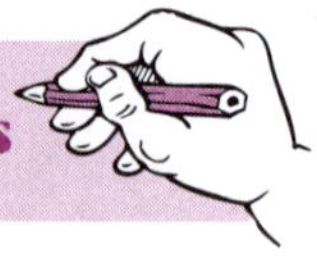

1. **Highlight** the **conjunction** that contrasts information.
2. **Circle** four **commas** that separate clauses in sentences.
3. **Underline** two **conjunctions**.
4. **Circle** the **comma** that separates a phrase from the rest of the sentence.
5. **Underline** the **prepositional phrase** that shows a contrast between the boys' homes.
6. **Circle** the **conjunction**.

Student B: Tahlia's draft

Tahlia, another Year 6 student, is going to **compare** and **contrast** the lives of Divya and Hayley. Divya is from Delhi, India, and Hayley lives on the Sunshine Coast in Australia.

Tahlia also starts by jotting down some notes about the girls.

Divya

- 12 years old—final year primary school—lives in Delhi, India—speaks English and Hindi fluently

School:
- starts at 8:30 am, ends at 2:30 pm
- subjects—e.g. English, Hindi, maths, science, history, geography, French, PE—taught in English

Home and family:
- lives in old, 3-bedroom house set in large garden
- lives with mother, father, older brother, younger sister
- no pets

Extra-curricular activities:
- extra maths tuition twice a week—spends about an hour on homework—does yoga, art, music (violin). Plays soccer and basketball for school teams

Ancestry:
- parents, grandparents and other ancestors born in India

Future goals:
- wants to be a history teacher

Hayley

- 12 years old—final year primary school—lives on Sunshine Coast, Australia—speaks English

School:
- starts at 9 am, ends at 3 pm
- subjects—e.g. English, maths, science, history, geography, art, music, computers and PE

Home and family:
- lives in modern, 4-bedroom house near beach
- lives with mother, father, older brother, younger sister
- 2 Maltese poodles (Bubbles and Popcorn)

Extra-curricular activities:
- spends about an hour doing homework—club netball—surf lifesaving (nipper)—dancing (ballet, jazz, tap)

Ancestry:
- father born in Ireland—mother's great-grandparents emigrated to Aus from England at end of 19th century

Future goals:
- wants to be a dance teacher

Help Tahlia sort out the similarities and differences between the girls' lives by completing the following table.

Differences: Divya	Similarities	Differences: Hayley

Writing the first draft

This is Tahlia's **first draft**. Read what she wrote and then answer the questions.

Divya and Hayley

Divya lives in Delhi in India and Hayley lives on the Sunshine Coast in Australia. They have just turned 12 and are in their final year of primary school.

The girls learn mainly the same subjects at school. Hayley and Divya both speak English, but she also speaks Hindi well. They spend about the same number of hours at school every day. They both do activities out of school. Divya does yoga and plays the violin. She plays soccer and basketball for her school. Hayley is a nipper at a surf lifesaving club and plays club netball. She goes to dancing three times a week and does ballet, jazz and tap. She wants to be a dance teacher one day. Divya wants to be a history teacher.

They both live in houses. Divya's house is old and has three bedrooms and a big garden. Hayley's house is modern and has four bedrooms and is near the beach. Divya and Hayley both have an older brother and a younger sister. Divya doesn't have any pets. Hayley has two Maltese poodles.

All of Divya's ancestors were born in India. Hayley's dad and her mum's great-grandparents emigrated to Australia from Ireland and England.

1. A text that **compares** and **contrasts** should contain the following features. Tick (✓) the ones that Tahlia has used in her draft.

   - **a** an **opening paragraph** that briefly states **who** or **what** is being **compared/ contrasted** ☐
   - **b** **middle paragraphs** that show **how** the subjects are **alike** or **different** ☐
   - **c** mainly **present-tense verbs** ☐
   - **d** **words** and **phrases** that express **comparison** and **contrast** ☐
   - **e** **correct spelling** and **punctuation** ☐
   - **f** a **conclusion** that **sums up** the information in the text by looking at both the **similarities** and **differences** between the subjects being compared and/or contrasted ☐

2. In what way are the extra-curricular activities you do similar to or different from those Divya and Hayley do?

   ____

   ____

   ____

3. In what way is your ancestry similar to or different from Divya's and Hayley's?

   ____

   ____

   ____

Step-by-step improvement plan

Like Josh, Tahlia has also identified the similarities and differences between Divya and Hayley's lives. However, she is going to do some practice exercises to find ways to make her text read more fluently. Help her complete the exercises.

Step 1: Use connectives that show similarity and difference

1. Join the following pairs of sentences with the **conjunction** in brackets.

   a The girls' way of life is different in many ways. They have some things in common. (although) ______________________________

   ____

   ____

   b Divya's school starts at 8:30 am and ends at 2:30 pm. Hayley's school starts at 9 am and ends at 3 pm. (while) ______________________________

   ____

   ____

   c Both girls learn English at school. Divya also learns Hindi. (but)

   ____

   ____

2. Complete the following paragraphs with an **adverb** or **prepositional phrase** from the box. Use each option once.

in addition	also	similarly	in contrast	however

The girls learn similar subjects at school and both are taught in English; ______________, Hindi, one of India's main languages, is ______________ an important subject at Divya's school.

As far as sport is concerned, Divya is good at soccer and basketball and plays for her school's teams. Hayley, ______________, is good at netball and plays for a club team. ______________, Hayley is a nipper at her local surf lifesaving club.

One of the most obvious differences between the two girls is in their ancestry. All of Divya's ancestors were born in India. Hayley's ancestors, ______________, come from Ireland and England.

3. Complete the following sentences using information from Tahlia's notes and draft.

   a Divya does not have a pet, whereas ______________________________

   ____

   b Unlike Divya, who lives in an old, ______________________________

   ____

   ____

Step 2: Use commas to separate words, phrases and clauses

Fill in the missing **commas** in the following sentences.

1. There are five people in each girl's family—a father mother and three children.
2. Divya speaks English and Hindi one of the main languages in India fluently.
3. Hayley on the other hand plays netball does surf lifesaving and goes to dancing.
4. While Divya and Hayley come from different parts of the world they share a number of similar experiences.
5. Hayley goes to dancing three times a week where she does ballet jazz and tap.

Step 3: Avoid making vague statements

A **vague statement** is one where the sentence's meaning is **unclear**.
For example: *Both Divya and Hayley have younger sisters, but* ***she*** *has a brother as well.*

The meaning of this sentence is **unclear** because the pronoun *she* can refer to either Divya or Hayley. In this case *she* should be replaced with the noun *Divya.*

1. Rewrite the following sentence so that the meaning is clearer.

   Although Divya and Hayley both live in houses, hers is more modern.

   ____

   ____

2. One of the sentences in Tahlia's draft contains a pronoun that can refer to either of the girls. Find the sentence and rewrite it so that the meaning is clear.

   ____

   ____

3. Rewrite the following sentence from Tahlia's draft so that the meaning is clear.

   Hayley's dad and her mum's great-grandparents emigrated to Australia from Ireland and England.

   ____

   ____

Step 4: Wrap up your comparison with a good conclusion

Tahlia's comparison does not include a summing up of the similarities and differences between Divya and Hayley's lives.

Help Tahlia write a good **concluding sentence** for her text that includes the following phrases.

comparison shows	from different countries	different customs and traditions	a number of similar experiences

____

____

____

Writing the final draft

Tahlia has started writing the **final draft** of her **comparison** of Divya and Hayley's lives. Help her complete it and then look in the answers section to compare what you have written with what Tahlia wrote.

Hint! Look at Tahlia's first draft and practice exercises for ideas.

Divya and Hayley

Divya and Hayley come from different parts of the world. Divya lives in Delhi, India and Hayley lives on the Sunshine Coast in Australia. Although the girls' way of life is different in many ways, they also have some things in common.

One way in which the girls' lives are similar is that both are in their final year at primary school and both have recently turned twelve. **(Continue the paragraph, telling how the girls' school experiences are similar and different.)**

....

....

....

....

....

....

Another similarity between the girls is that they both take part in a number of extra-curricular activities, although the types of activities they do are different. Divya does yoga and goes to violin lessons. She also plays soccer and basketball for her school. Hayley, on the other hand, plays netball for a club and is a nipper at her local surf lifesaving club. She also goes to dancing three times a week, where she does ballet, jazz and tap.

The girls' families are also similar in some ways. **(Continue the paragraph, telling how the girls' families and homes are similar and different.)**

....

....

....

....

....

....

One of the most obvious differences between the two girls is in their ancestry. Divya's parents, grandparents and other ancestors were all born in India. In contrast, Hayley's father was born in Ireland and her mother's great-grandparents emigrated to Australia from England at the end of the 19th century. **(Write a good conclusion.)**

Your turn

Write a text of one to two pages on one of the following. Use your own paper for this activity.

Writing Checklist Make sure your text includes: ✓

- an **opening paragraph** that briefly states **who** or **what** is being **compared** and/or **contrasted**. ☐
- **middle paragraphs** that show **how** the subjects are **alike or different**. ☐
- mainly **present-tense verbs**. ☐
- **words** and **phrases** that express **comparison** and **contrast**. ☐
- **correct spelling** and **punctuation**. ☐
- a **conclusion** that **sums up** the information in the text by looking at both the **similarities** and **differences** between the subjects being compared and/or contrasted. ☐

Tip Use **Josh's final draft** on page 102 and **Tahlia's final draft** on page 107 to help you.

Go to **WORD BANK** page 122 for useful vocabulary

Compare and contrast one of the following:

- life in the city and life in the country
- buses and trains
- hats and umbrellas
- books and newspapers
- wood and plastic
- two of your friends or relatives
- bees and butterflies

Answers

Unit 1 Factual recounts—newspaper reports

Page 1

1 a and d 2 b

Page 2

1 Nottingham 2 Richard Morgan
3 Meander Falls, Alum Cliffs, Launceston
4 Dr Daniel Sutton
5 the Parks and Wildlife Service

Page 3

1 c, d, e, f, g
2 a is, says, need b knew, had

Pages 4–5

Step 1

1 b
2 **Suggestion:** ALIVE AFTER 10 DAYS IN BUSH

Step 2

1 Richard Morgan, a British backpacker, who was last seen in the Meander Falls area on 6 August, has been found by two bushwalkers.
2 Mr Morgan, who is believed to have spent the last ten days in the bush, is now recovering in Launceston General Hospital.

Step 3

1 Doctor Daniel Sutton says Mr Morgan will remain in hospital until at least Sunday.
"We need to carry out some precautionary tests," he said.
2 George Lumley, regional manager of the Parks and Wildlife Service, said Mr Morgan obviously had some bush craft skills.
"He knew to stay warm and dry," he said.

Step 4

1 Mr Morgan, 20, of Nottingham, went missing from his backpackers' hostel on 6 August.
2 Mr Morgan's parents were due to fly to Australia when they received a text message informing them that Mr Morgan had been found alive and well.

Page 6

1 Richard Morgan, Meander Falls 2 has spent
3 "We need to carry out some precautionary tests before we release him,"
4 rugged, unfamiliar 5 has, are
6 he was heading to the Alum Cliffs area
7 Nottingham, Australia

Page 7

Suggestion: Jayden should use the photograph of the water-bombing helicopter because he mentions two of them in his notes. His notes don't say anything about a house being destroyed.

Page 8

1 c, d, e, f, g
2 a blaze b feared for c contain

Pages 9–10

Step 1

1 **Suggestion:** a, c
2 BUSHFIRE RAGING OUT OF CONTROL

Step 2

1 A large bushfire south of Adelaide has destroyed sheds, crops and livestock.
2 The fire started at about 10 am yesterday on a property 70 km south of Adelaide. Farmer Mike Bailey said he feared for his cattle after flames came within 50 m of his home.

Step 3

1 "I've managed to move some of the cattle, but I've lost one of the paddocks," said Mike Bailey.
2 "The hot, dry conditions are making it difficult for firefighters to contain the blaze," said Lorenzo Russo.

Step 4

1 A Country Fire Service spokesperson said sixty firefighters and two water-bombing helicopters had so far been unable to bring the blaze under control.
2 a Lorenzo Russo, of the Bureau of Meteorology, said the situation should start to ease tomorrow when a cool change blows in.
b Much-needed rain is expected to fall over the area, bringing welcome relief to weary firefighters.

Page 11

A large bushfire south of Adelaide has destroyed sheds, crops and livestock.

The fire started at about 10 am yesterday on a property 70 km south of Adelaide. Farmer Mike Bailey said he feared for his cattle after flames came within 50 m of his home. "We've managed to move some of them, but we've lost one of the paddocks," he said.

A Country Fire Service spokesperson said sixty firefighters and two water-bombing helicopters had so far been unable to bring the blaze under control.

Lorenzo Russo of the Bureau of Meteorology said,

"The hot, dry conditions are making it difficult for the firefighters to contain the blaze. But the situation should start to ease tomorrow when a cool change blows in."

Much-needed rain is expected to fall over the area, bringing welcome relief to weary firefighters.

Unit 2 Restaurant reviews

Page 13

1 a, c, d

2 a cosy b comfortable c delicious d dry

Page 14

1 a crunchy and chewy b sweet and creamy c cool and refreshing

2 c

3 **Suggestion:** On the menu were items such as pizza, ice cream/gelato and fresh fruit juice.

Page 15

1 b, d, e

2 a an entrée b a snack c à la carte d seasoning

Pages 16–17

Step 1

1 **Suggestion:** On Wednesday I went with a group of Year 6s to Molto Delizioso, the new Italian restaurant near our school. They wanted us to try their menu and give suggestions on how they could improve the restaurant.

2 **Suggestion:** The owners of Molto Delizioso, the new Italian restaurant near our school, recently invited some students to try their new menu and give suggestions on how they could improve the restaurant. I went with a group of Year 6s last Wednesday.

Step 2

1 a weird, delicious/heavenly
b freshly squeezed, ice-cold, refreshing

2 a The pizza crust was thin and crisp.
b The banana split pizza tasted heavenly/delicious.
c I thought the music was a bit old-fashioned.
d I thought the service was outstanding.

Step 3

1 ladled/drizzled 2 coated 3 sprinkled 4 drizzled/ladled 5 garnished

Step 4

Suggestion: I will definitely tell my parents about Molto Delizioso. They have an excellent menu, with some healthy choices. Our waiter told us that Molto Delizioso means very delicious in Italian, and that's just what their food is—very delicious!

Page 18

1 the new Italian restaurant near our school
2 delicious 3 sprinkled, drizzled
4 fresh orange, apple and pineapple juice
5 old-fashioned 6 very delicious

Page 19

1 **Meat and Poultry**
Spicy Chicken Cacciatore Braised Lamb Shanks
Beef Braciole
Italian Sausage, Peppers and Onions

Vegetarian
Mushroom Risotto Zucchini Fries
Baked Eggplant

Dessert
Almond Cheesecake Raspberry Panna Cotta
Double Chocolate Biscotti

2 **Suggestion:** If I had to choose three items from the above menu, they would be Braised Lamb Shanks, Mushroom Risotto and Raspberry Panna Cotta.

Page 20

1 a, b, d, e 2 sample 3 decorated 4 survey

Pages 21–22

Step 1

Suggestions:

1 The restaurant is decorated in green, white and red, which are the colours of the Italian flag.

2 I knew the sauce had been made with fresh tomatoes because I cook a lot with Mum at home and we often make Napolitana sauce.

3 My apple juice, which had been freshly squeezed, was also good./My apple juice had been freshly squeezed and was also good.

4 I've been to lots of Italian restaurants, but/and this one definitely has the best choice of food.

Step 2

1 a bright, happy b tasty c divine d amazing e mouth-watering

2 **Suggestions:**
a The Pasta Napolitana was tasteless and boring.
b The dessert was dry and unappealing.

Step 3

1 a swirl of cream 2 A ripple of raspberry
3 a splash of oil
4 a scattering of finely chopped herbs
5 a light dusting of icing sugar

Page 23

On Wednesday some Year 6 students were invited to sample the menu at Molto Delizioso, the new Italian restaurant near our school. I was lucky enough to be one of them.

The restaurant is decorated in green, white and red, which are the colours of the Italian flag. The walls are painted red and white and the tablecloths are green and white. To add to the Italian atmosphere, there are pictures of Italy everywhere. The bright colours made me feel happy straight away.

I started with the Pasta Napoletana. I could tell that the pasta sauce had been made with fresh tomatoes because I cook a lot with Mum at home and we often make Napoletana sauce. The pasta was perfect—not too hard and not too mushy. Our waiter told us the word for that is *al dente*.

For dessert I had the Cannoli with Vanilla Custard. It was topped off with a swirl of cream and a light dusting of icing sugar. There is only one word to describe it—divine! My freshly squeezed apple juice was also amazing.

I've been to lots of Italian restaurants, but this one definitely has the best choice of food. There is something for everyone on the menu, including many unusual items such as taco pizza and a variety of mouth-watering dessert pizzas.

When it came to filling in the questionnaire at the end of the meal, I gave Molto Delizioso five stars for their friendly waiters, excellent service and delicious food.

Unit 3 Descriptions—photographs

Page 25

1 a narrative b information report c poem
2 a

Page 26

1 a the fir trees b the olive trees
c the road d the mountains e the shadows
2 a the mountains b the fir trees

Page 27

1 a, b, c, f, g
2 a shorter, puffy b uneven
c magnificent d magical
3 **Suggestion:** On the morning I took this photograph everything before me was beautiful and in harmony.

Pages 28–29

Step 1

1 a pools b long fingers c a checkerboard
d benches e slate
2 a were shimmering sequins b were ghosts
3 **Suggestion:** The trees formed a series of full stops and exclamation marks along the side of the road.

Step 2

1 a fingers b danced
c nodded politely to each other
2 a The sun gazed down at the scene below, showering it with light.
b The mountain lay quietly in the background, covered in a coat of green.

Step 3

1 lay 2 created 3 cast 4 hooked
5 swayed 6 etched 7 skirted, conjured

Page 30

1 harmony, beauty, surroundings
2 like a series of full stops and exclamation marks like sentinels on guard
3 trying to stamp their authority on it, hooking themselves over the hedge, like long thin fingers
4 swayed, nodded, etched 5 pools of shadow

Page 31

1 c 2 b
3 The cars that carry people up and down the mountain travel along the cables.

Page 32

1 a, b, c, f, g
2 Literally he was standing high up, looking down at the world below, and figuratively it would have made him feel good.
3 fragile

Pages 33–34

Step 1

1 a an abstract painting b narrow ribbons
c a spider's web d a fortress
e a huge whale
2 a Far below me lay buildings and playing fields, arranged like an abstract painting.
b The cables along which the cars travelled were stretched tautly, looking as fragile as a spider's web.
c The cables disappeared into a sturdy building that stood like a fortress on solid rock.
3 **Suggestions:**
a The roads looked like narrow ribbons winding round the mountain.
b The island looked like a huge whale spouting water from its blowhole.
4 a a sheet of tranquil blue b a fine mist
c **Suggestion**: In the distance the ocean was a sheet of tranquil blue, with smoke like a fine mist drifting from an island close to shore.

Step 2

1 b 2 a cloak
3 **Suggestions:**
a The rocky outcrop scanned the horizon, like an ancient Egyptian pharaoh surveying his kingdom.
b The rocky outcrop scanned the horizon, like an ancient Egyptian pharaoh, his cloak falling in soft folds about him.

Step 3

1 a speckled b threaded c strung
d spouting e drifted f gazed
2 a, b, e

Page 35

On the day I took this photograph I was feeling on top of the world—literally because I was standing on top of a mountain looking down on the world, and figuratively because I was excited to be there.

Far below me buildings and playing fields speckled the landscape, like an abstract painting, and roads threaded their way across the open countryside, like narrow ribbons. The cables along which the car travels up and down the mountain were strung tautly, looking as fragile as a spider's web against the backdrop of the blue water. They disappeared into a sturdy building that stood fortress-like on solid rock.

In the distance, the ocean was a sheet of tranquil blue. An island, like a giant whale, rose from its depths, spouting a fine mist from its blowhole. Two boats closer to shore drifted lazily on the still water, apparently unconcerned by the threat the creature might pose.

A rocky outcrop on the mountain below gazed serenely out to sea, like an ancient pharaoh surveying his kingdom, with his cloak swirling about him.

Now, whenever I feel downcast, all I have to do to recapture the sense of elation I experienced that day is look at this photograph.

Unit 4 Expositions—editorials

Page 37

1 b 2 b

3 **Suggestion:** I chose statement **b** because it says I *must* read the book. The word *must* is very strong and makes me feel that I have to read the book. It also says the book is *fantastic*, which makes it sound really special.

Page 38

Suggestion:

Argument 3: During wars, innocent people get injured and killed. They could lose their homes and all their possessions if they are forced to flee. They aren't able to lead normal lives because they live in a state of fear.

Page 39

1 **a, b, c, d, f, h, i**

2 **Suggestions:**

- a People who respect those who are different from them in some way definitely wouldn't be unkind to them.
- b One of the main reasons for wars is that some people don't respect the right of others to follow their own religion or culture.

Pages 40–41

Step 1

1 When people do not respect the rights of others, it can cause many problems. Bullying, for example, is a big problem in many schools. It is also a problem in our school. It can have serious consequences for both the bullies and their victims. Crime, too, can affect people badly. On the one hand, the victims of crime can become extremely frightened; on the other hand, the criminals can end up spending time in jail.

2 a However, So
  b also, for instance, Moreover

Step 2

1 a probably/perhaps/possibly
  b Maybe/Perhaps c definitely/certainly

2 **Suggestions:**

- a Clearly, bullying will only stop being a problem when people start to respect those who are different from them in some way.
- b We would definitely have fewer wars if people had more respect for other people's religions and way of life.
- c I strongly believe that if people are taught to respect others and their property, there will be less crime in the world.

Step 3

1 a pretty, beautiful, breath-taking
  b ugly, hideous, grotesque
  c large, enormous, massive
  d horrible, gruesome, spine-chilling

2 a suffering/misery b miserable/unbearable
  c terrified d destroy/ruin e terrible

Page 42

1 This is not always the case, but I strongly believe that if people learn to respect the rights of others, the world will be a safer place.

2 for example, also, However 3 while

4 On the one hand, on the other hand 5 clearly

6 Both sentences refer back to the arguments.

Page 43

Suggestions:

1 We can use public transport more often. We can walk if we are only travelling a short distance. We can ride a bicycle to school or work.

2 We can switch off lights when we don't need them. We can spend less time in the shower. When not using them, we can switch off electrical appliances like kettles at the power point.

Page 44

1 **a, b, c, d, f, h, i, j**

2 **Suggestions:**

- a People can help reduce air pollution by using less electricity and being more careful about the way they use their cars.
- b Water becomes polluted when people leave their rubbish lying around and items like plastic bags get washed into waterways.

Pages 45–46

Step 1

Suggestion: One of the biggest problems in the world today is pollution. In many places the air, water and soil are so polluted that they cause diseases in plants, animals and humans. I believe that the only way to help prevent pollution is for us all to start taking better care of the environment.

Step 2

Suggestions:

1. Air pollution can irritate people's throats, eyes and noses and give them asthma.
2. Things we can do to help prevent air pollution are to use our cars less and to use less electricity.
3. Sometimes the soil gets polluted when people use chemicals on plants to kill insects and weeds.
4. Chemicals from landfills that get into the soil can affect plants.
5. The need for clean air, clean water and food free from poisons are important reasons for taking care of the environment.

Step 3

1. **a** for example **b** However, also
   c In the meantime **d** therefore
   e otherwise
2. **Suggestions:**

a We can help the environment by not using our cars all the time; instead, we can use public transport more often or walk to school or work.

b Pollution can cause health problems in humans; therefore it is important that we all start taking better care of the environment.

Step 4

1 spew, noxious **2** toxic **3** huge
4 severe **5** healthier
6 filthy, thick with, polluted

Page 47

Why it is important to care for the environment

One of the biggest problems in the world today is pollution. In many places the air, water and soil are so polluted that they cause diseases in plants, animals and humans. I believe that the only way to help prevent pollution is for us all to start taking better care of the environment.

Air pollution, for example, can cause respiratory diseases such as asthma. It can also irritate people's throats and make their eyes and noses burn. These problems can eventually lead to more serious health issues. Many organisations are trying to find ways of producing clean energy, but in the meantime, we can help reduce air pollution by, for example, using less electricity in our homes and using public transport or cycling or walking to school or work. If we all start caring for the environment in a small way, I am convinced we can make a difference.

Water pollution also causes health problems in humans. Polluted water contains viruses and bacteria and if people drink it, they can get diseases such as typhoid. However, polluted water also kills plants and animals such as fish. People often leave their empty packets, cans and bottles lying around outside. Many of these objects, especially plastic bags, end up in streams, rivers and eventually the ocean. Animals die when they get caught in the bags or try to eat them. If we are all more careful about the way we dispose of our waste, I am certain our rivers and oceans will become less polluted.

Finally, soil pollution is a problem for humans, animals and plants. The soil becomes polluted when chemicals and other poisons seep into the earth. The chemicals could come from landfills or from pesticides and herbicides that people use on plants.

If people and animals eat the plants grown in polluted soil, they can become ill or even die. The chemicals can also end up destroying the natural vegetation. All of us therefore need to be more careful about the way we care for our plants and dispose of our waste.

The need for clean air, clean water and food free from poisons is obviously an important reason why we should care for the environment. However, we should also remember that Earth is our home. We have nowhere else to go. We therefore have no choice but to look after it.

Unit 5 Explanations

Page 49

1 **b** **2** **a, c, d, f**
3 **c** = 1; **a** = 2; **d** = 3; **b** = 4

Page 50

1. Sunlight is renewable and it is free.
2. Some places in the world don't receive much sunlight, and even in sunny areas the sun doesn't shine at night or on cloudy days.

Page 51

1. **a, b, c, f, h, j**
2. In case you didn't know, Anyway

Pages 52–53

Step 1

1 **c** **2** **b**

Step 2

1. The word *solar* comes from the Latin word *sol*, which means sun.

2 Solar energy is the energy we get from sunlight, which all living things need to survive.
3 The panels that produce heat are called thermal panels, while/and those that generate electricity are called photovoltaic (PV) panels.

Step 3

1 a Sunlight can be turned into heat and electricity.
b The electric currents are captured by/in an electrical circuit.
c Solar panels should be tilted at an angle.
2 a Using solar energy to produce electricity has major advantages.
b Producing electricity from solar energy does not cause air pollution.

Page 54

1 which 2 harnessed, converted, generate
3 These currents are then captured in an electrical circuit 4 so 5 However, therefore

Page 55

1 a to dry our washing, cool down our houses and other buildings.
b to turn the blades of windmills on farms.
c to move boats like yachts.
2 The generator causes electrons in magnets inside wire coils to move, and an electric current starts to flow.

Page 56

1 a, b, c, g, i, j
2 a ventilate b rotate c to drive

Pages 57–58

Step 1

1 b
2 a People have been using the wind's energy for centuries.
b The wind's energy can be turned into electricity using wind turbines.

Step 2

1 For centuries, people have been using the wind's energy to move ships across rivers and oceans and to ventilate their homes and buildings.
2 They have built windmills that have allowed them to grind grain and to pump water mechanically.
3 More recently, people have started harnessing the wind's energy in a turbine, which is a machine that spins around in a fast-moving flow of air, steam, gas, water or other fluid.
4 The magnets inside the coils of wire start to move when electrons break free from the metal and start to flow.
5 Many people think that wind farms are ugly and that they spoil the landscape, while some people who live close to wind farms complain of the noise emitted by the turbines.

Step 3

1 a The wind's energy can be harnessed to produce electricity.
b The wind's energy is converted into electricity in large machines called turbines.
c Wind turbines are mounted on very tall towers.
d Lots of turbines are needed to generate enough electricity to power people's homes and other buildings.
2 The generator behind the gearbox is driven by the rotating drive shaft.

Page 59

How we get electricity from wind energy

People have been making practical use of the wind's energy for centuries. They have used it to move ships across rivers and oceans and to ventilate homes and other buildings. They have also built windmills that allowed them to grind grain and pump water mechanically, tasks that windmills perform to this day.

More recently, the wind's energy has been harnessed to produce electricity. This is done using a turbine, which is a machine that spins around in a fast-moving flow of air (such as on a windmill), steam, gas, water or other fluid.

Wind turbines are mounted on very tall towers. Each turbine consists of three rotors (blades), a gearbox and a generator attached to a drive shaft. When the wind blows, the rotor blades start to spin, causing the drive shaft to start rotating slowly. The gearbox then increases the speed of rotation from 16 revolutions per minute (rpm) to 1600 rpm. This is enough to drive the generator behind the gearbox.

On the rotating shaft in the gearbox are magnets and coils of wire. When the magnets inside the coils of wire are moved, electrons (tiny pieces of electricity) break free from the metal and start to flow, resulting in an electric current.

Using wind power instead of fossil fuels to create electricity has advantages and disadvantages. On the positive side, it is a renewable energy source and it does not cause pollution. On the negative side, many people think that wind turbines are ugly and spoil the landscape, while some people who live close to wind farms complain of the noise emitted by the turbines. The rotating blades are also a danger to birds. On the whole, however, wind power is a much cleaner source of energy than fossil fuels.

Unit 6 Narratives

Page 61

1 Answers will vary.
2 **Suggestions:** a fantasy, adventure
b legend, myth c science fiction, adventure

3 Answers will vary. **Suggestions:**
- a The Invisible Boy/Girl
- b Prometheus and the Gift of Fire
- c Mission to Mars

Page 62

1 **Suggestions:**
- a "Dad! Grandpa! Come and watch me ride my bike!"
- b "That's my boy! I knew you could do it!"
- c "Good job, Tom! I'm really proud of you."

Page 63

1 a, b, c, d, e, f, i, j   2 a

Pages 64–65

Step 1

1 **Suggestions:** a a beast   b a shell

2 **Suggestions:**
- a The bike stood at the back of the shed, like a beast waiting to pounce on me.
- b The helmet was as snug as a shell on my head.

3 **Suggestions:** a a dark purple flower
- b scribbles

4 **Suggestions:**
- a A bruise was starting to blossom on his leg.
- b Scrapes and scratches formed little scribbles on his knees and elbows.

5 a, c and e

Step 2

Suggestions: 1 lounging   2 gleaming
3 tormented   4 spurred

Step 3

1 Dad's words tormented him all day and were like a thorn festering inside his flesh, but they spurred him into action.

2 He was balanced. He was in control. The bike was obeying him.

Page 66

1 sparks of light gleaming on it silver handlebars, <u>like eyes winking at him</u>, mocking him

2 humiliated

3 He would conquer the beast.   4 firmly

5 A bruise was blossoming on his leg and scrapes and scratches formed little scribbles on his knees and elbows.

6 He was balanced. The bike was obeying him. He had conquered the beast!

Page 67

Suggestions:

1 "I've got some wonderful news, Lucy! I've been promoted! It means we'll have to move to Melbourne, but I know you'll love it there."

2 "But that means I'll have to go to a new school. I'll be leaving all my friends."

3 "This is Lucinda, class. I know you will all do whatever you can to make her feel welcome and to help her settle in."

4 I think I would feel just like Lucinda. I would be really nervous because I wouldn't know anyone or what to expect.

Page 68

1 a, b, c, d, e, h, i, j

2 **Suggestions:**
- a Lucinda felt sad when she heard that they'd be moving to another city.
- b When Mum asked Lucinda about her new school, Lucinda said, "It wasn't as bad as I thought it would be. I like my teacher and I've already made some friends."

Pages 69–70

Step 1

1 a kitten (simile)   b sea (metaphor)
- c jelly (simile)

2 **Suggestions:**
- a Lucinda had known everyone at her old school, but now she was in alien territory and she was terrified.
- b As Lucinda looked at the strange faces around her, she felt like a fish out of water.
- c The day Lucinda heard that they'd be moving to another city, her world fell apart.

Step 2

1 Personal preference—they are all good choices.

2 a cast   b gathered   c cut
- d wrapped, notice   e raced

3 **Suggestions:**
- a Lucinda's legs trembled as she waited with Mum on the playground.
- b When someone asked her about her old school, Lucinda mumbled a reply.

Step 3

1 **Suggestions:**
- a All the other kids on the playground knew each other and suddenly she felt very lonely.
- b Now, as Lucinda stood on the playground, a string of questions tumbled through her head.
- c She was so wrapped up in her own little world that she didn't notice a tall girl with dark hair approaching her until a friendly voice cut into her thoughts.
- d However, Lucinda needn't have worried as her teacher was kind and caring and Lucinda liked her immediately.

2 a The knot in her stomach grew tighter. Her legs felt like jelly. This was unknown territory.
- b Lucinda asked herself lots of questions. Would the other students like her? Would she like them?

Page 71

The New School

Lucinda wanted to clutch her mum's hand as they walked through the gates, but she didn't dare. She cast her eyes nervously around the playground. Students were gathered in little clusters, talking and laughing happily together. The knot in her stomach grew tighter. Her legs felt like jelly. This was unknown territory, and she was the alien.

Not so long ago things had been different. She'd been popular at her old school and had always been surrounded by familiar faces. Her life had been perfect. But that had all changed the day her mother had announced that she'd been promoted and they'd be moving to another city. Mum was enthusiastic about their new life, but Lucinda felt as though her world had fallen apart.

The thing Lucinda had dreaded the most about their move was going to a new school. Now, as she stood on the playground, a string of questions tumbled through her head. Would the other students like her? Would her teachers like her? Would she like them? She was so wrapped up in her own little world that she didn't notice a tall girl with dark hair approaching her. A friendly voice cut into her thoughts.

"Hello," said the voice, "you must be Lucinda. I'm Alex. Come and join us."

Lucinda quickly said goodbye to her mum and followed Alex to one of the groups she'd spotted earlier. Alex introduced her to the other students in the group. They smiled at her and asked her questions about her old school. Then just as she started to relax, Lucinda remembered it would soon be time to face the next challenge—meeting her teacher. But she needn't have worried. Miss Roberts was kind and caring and Lucinda liked her immediately.

When the home time bell rang at three o'clock, Lucinda breathed a sigh of relief. She'd made it through the first day, and it hadn't been as bad as she'd feared. She liked her teacher, she liked the school, and she'd even made some new friends. A little quiver of excitement raced up her spine. Suddenly she was looking forward to her new life.

Unit 7 Poetry—free verse poems

Page 73

1 c

2 **Suggestion:** It rained hard today. The leaves were wet and the clouds were heavy. The ferns on the riverbank gleamed in the faint light, while the river tossed and swirled as it rolled relentlessly across the open plain.

Page 74

1 b

2 The *s* sound mimics the hissing of a snake. It is also the shape a snake makes as it slithers along the ground.

3 a fissure b slackness c vaguely
d flickered e mused f stooped

Page 75

1 a 2 b

Pages 76–77

Step 1

1 a bobbed or rocked b expertly or properly
c tug or drag d flapping or struggling
e flimsy or slim f protruding or bulging
g grotesquely or monstrously

2 a nestling b zoomed c snatched
d caressed e flicked

Step 2

1 a We sailed quickly out to sea.
b But then I felt something pull on the line.
c Its scales were shiny
d its eyes were huge
e I knew the air would kill it

2 **Suggestions:**
a My heart was pounding.
b Its fins were as flimsy as paper.
c I saluted it.

Step 3

1 a flimsy feather floated, fan
b proud peacock, plumage
c big blue ball bounced
d cheeky children chattered
e runners, red ribbons

2 **Suggestions:**
a silver, sped, sea b bobbing, soft
c fishing, folded, fingers
d flimsy, fans e Silently, sea

Page 78

1 like a mast without a sail 2 sped, bobbing
3 Heart pounding
4 flapping furiously, Silver scales sparkling sunlight, Fins flimsy fans
5 I saluted him

Page 79

1 He compares them to people sewing the shadows together with spools of dark thread.
2 He likes them and enjoys watching them flying about.
3 *disgustingly* and *disgusting*.

Page 80

1 a 2 furious
3 a expectation to disappointment
b surprise to acceptance
c anxiety to relief

Pages 81–82

Step 1

1 a scattered b marched c sobbing d buried e cradled

2 **Suggestions:**
 a I was so livid I could feel my blood start to boil.
 b I raged madly at her.
 c Her face was all puckered and red from crying.
 d She was cowering in fear at my feet.
 e Her voice trembled when she said she was sorry.

Step 2

1 a tells b shows c tells d shows e shows f tells g tells h shows i shows j tells

2 b She was embarrassed. c She was angry. d She was sad. e She was frightened.

Step 3

1 a a bird trapped in a cage
 b a startled rabbit
 c a poisonous liquid
 d a volcano about to erupt
 e mice gnawing on a rope
 f ice touched by the sun's warmth

2 **Suggestions:** a fear b surprise

3 **Suggestions:** a wings b petals c pools

Page 83

Necklace

My little sister broke my red necklace
Beads scattered across the floor
like tiny drops of blood
my blood boiling
I called her names
I raged madly.
I marched into her room
Hands on hips, arms
Jutting out like wings.
She was sitting on the floor—crying, sobbing
Face buried in her hands
hands as soft and delicate as petals.
She heard me and looked up
Face all puckered and red
Tear-stained cheeks
Eyes filled with fear.
My heart lurched,
Hard cold heart
Melted,
Like ice touched by the sun's warmth.
I sat down beside her and
cradled her in my arms.

Unit 8 Biographies

Page 85

1 Arun was born in a small country town on 1 January. His parents named him Arun, which means 'dawn' in Hindi, for several reasons: he was their first child; they had only recently arrived in Australia from India; and he had come into the world on the first day of the new millennium. His name therefore symbolised a number of new beginnings for them.

2 **Suggestion:** William Henry Gates was born on 28 October 1955 in Seattle in the United States of America. He is the only son of William and Mary Gates and has an older and a younger sister.

Page 86

1 It would have brought more money into the colony.

2 People from all around the world came to Australia in search of gold, so it led to an increase in the population. The population also became more multicultural.

Page 87

1 a, b, c, d, f, g

2 **Suggestion:**
 a Elizabeth Macarthur was born in Devon, England on 14 August 1766.
 b Elizabeth came to Australia with her husband, John, in 1790.

Pages 88–89

Step 1

John and Elizabeth Macarthur arrived in Sydney in June 1790. Shortly afterwards John was granted 100 acres of land in Parramatta. He called the property Elizabeth Farm. Today Elizabeth Farm is a museum.

John Macarthur bought his first merino sheep in 1796. He and Elizabeth worked hard to build up their flocks and soon they had almost 4000 almost-pure merinos.

John was an argumentative man. After arguing with the governor, he was forced to return to England. He stayed there for nine years. During that time Elizabeth managed the flocks, with great success. By the time John returned, the wool industry in New South Wales was well established.

Step 2

1 Western Australia
 The Man from Snowy River
 Caroline Chisholm College
 Mother Teresa Primary School
 National Gallery of Australia
 Queen Victoria Museum and Art Gallery
 University of the Sunshine Coast

2 **Corrections:** Elizabeth Farm Camden Park New South Wales

Step 3

1 a positive b negative c positive d positive e negative

2 **Suggestions:**
 a Elizabeth helped her husband by managing their farms and flocks while he was in England.
 b Elizabeth Macarthur played an important role in establishing the wool industry in New South Wales.

Page 90

1 Elizabeth Macarthur, Devon, England, August, Australia, John, June
2 Shortly after arriving in New South Wales, Today, In 1805 3 very good
4 argumentative, clashed, quarrelled
5 However, he could never have achieved his success without Elizabeth's help and support.

Page 91

1 **Suggestion:** Early aeroplanes had open cockpits, so pilots needed goggles and leather helmets for protection and warmth.
2 adventurous, courageous, determined

Page 92

1 **a, b, c, d, f, g**
2 Charles Kingsford Smith was born in Brisbane on 9 February 1897. He was the seventh child of William Smith, a banker, and Mary Kingsford.
3 **Suggestion:** The aircraft today are bigger and more powerful and they can travel a lot faster.

Pages 93–94

Step 1

When he was a child, Charles Kingsford Smith's family spent four years in Canada. When they returned to Australia, Charles completed his education in Sydney. During the First World War, Charles fought at Gallipoli and in Egypt and France. He started training as a pilot and was made a lieutenant after being awarded the Military Cross for bravery. After the war Charles continued to fly planes. First he worked as a stunt flier in a circus in the United States, and then he joined a joy-riding company in Sydney.

Step 2

Southern Cross, Sydney Airport, St Andrew's Cathedral School, Sydney Technical High School, Interstate Flying Services

Step 3

1 a In 1916 he started training as a pilot and was appointed a flying officer the following year.
 b Charles formed his own flying company, Interstate Flying Services, with two other pilots.
 c In 1930 Charles launched Australian National Airways and completed a crossing from Ireland to Newfoundland in 31½ hours.
2 a Later that year Charles flew solo from England to Darwin in the record-breaking time of less than10 days.
 b On 6 November 1935 Charles and another pilot took off from England to try for another record-breaking flight to Australia, but their plane crashed into the sea and both pilots were lost.

Step 4

Suggestion: Australia has recognised Charles Kingsford Smith's contribution to aviation by naming Sydney Airport after him. He was also once featured on the Australian $20 note.

Page 95

Sir Charles Kingsford Smith

Charles Kingsford Smith, a pioneer of aviation in Australia, was born on 9 February 1897 in Brisbane. He was the seventh child of William Smith, a banker, and Mary Kingsford. His family spent four years in Canada when he was a child, but they returned to Sydney in 1907. Charles completed his education in Sydney at St Andrew's Cathedral School and later at Sydney Technical High School.

During the First World War, Charles fought at Gallipoli and in Egypt and France. In 1916 he started training as a pilot and was appointed a flying officer the following year. He became a lieutenant after being awarded the Military Cross for bravery.

Charles continued to fly planes after the war. First he worked as a stunt flier in a circus in the United States, and then he joined a joy-riding company in Sydney. He also worked as a pilot for Western Australian Airways for a while. However, he wanted to start his own flying company, and, together with two other pilots, formed Interstate Flying Services. In order to raise money, Charles and one of his partners completed some important demonstration flights. They flew around Australia in a time of10 days and 5 hours, and from California to Brisbane in the *Southern Cross* in 83 hours and 38 minutes.

In 1930 Charles launched Australian National Airways and completed a trans-Atlantic crossing from Ireland to Newfoundland in 31½ hours. Later that year he flew solo from England to Darwin in a record-breaking time of just less than 10 days. He was knighted for his services to aviation in 1932.

On 6 November 1935 Charles and another pilot took off from England to try for another record-breaking flight to Australia. Their plane, however, crashed into the sea and both pilots were lost.

In recognition of Charles Kingsford Smith's contribution to aviation in Australia, Sydney's airport was named after him and he was once featured on the Australian $20 note.

Unit 9 Compare and contrast texts

Page 97

1 **Suggestion:** While there are similarities between nests and houses, there are also differences.

They are similar because **both offer shelter and both have to be built**. The main reason they are different is that **animals live in nests and humans live in houses**.

2 **Suggestions**
Similarities—both are mammals; both are kept as pets; both are covered in fur
Differences—dogs are generally bigger than cats; they make different sounds; cats can jump higher than dogs

Page 98

Differences: Shunyuan	Similarities	Differences: Owen
lives in China—speaks Mandarin	Both:	lives in England—speaks English—can't speak Mandarin
has a longer school day—lots more homework	are 11 years old, in final year of primary school	shorter school day—gets less homework
PE—daily group exercises with flag-raising ceremony and singing of national anthem	do similar subjects at school	PE—twice a week—do exercises and play games (soccer, cricket)
only child—lives in apartment in high-rise—no pets	do exercises during PE	has a younger brother and sister—lives in a house with a garden—has 2 pets
not much time for leisure activities	play soccer	has time for leisure activities—TV, computer games, soccer, cricket
wants to work with animals	understand English	wants to be a vet
	live with mother and father	
	want to work with animals one day	

Page 99

1 a, b, c, e
2 **Suggestion:** My home is similar to Owen's. I also live in a three-bedroom, double-storey house, and like Owen, I live with my mother, father, brother and sister. However, I only have one pet—a Chihuahua named Charlie.

Pages 100–101

Step 1

1 a although/but/yet
b Although/Even though
c while/whereas
d Even though/Although/While
e whereas/while/but

2 The students at Shunyuan's school do group exercises every day. The students at Owen's school do exercises during PE; however, they also play games like soccer and cricket.

3 a on the other hand/in contrast
b in contrast/on the other hand
c in comparison to

Step 2

1 maths, science, geography and history
his mum, dad, brother, sister and two pets
Yes, Josh has used commas correctly.

2 a Both Shunyuan and Owen live with their parents, but whereas Shunyuan is an only child, Owen has a younger brother and sister.
b Both boys learn maths, science, history, geography and art, but while Owen's main language is English, Shunyuan's is Mandarin.

3 **Suggestions:**
a In his spare time, Owen watches TV, plays computer games and plays cricket and soccer.
b Three subjects that both boys do at school are maths, science and PE, while the subject Shunyuan does that Owen doesn't do is Mandarin.

Step 3

Text a.

Page 102

1 Although
2 Both boys learn maths, science, history, geography and art, but while Owen's main language is English, Shunyuan's is Mandarin. Shunyuan can communicate in English, as he does it as a second language at school, but Owen doesn't know any Mandarin.
3 and, but
4 Unlike Shunyuan,
5 on the other hand
6 even though

Page 103

Differences: Divya	Similarities	Differences: Hayley
lives in India—can speak Hindi	Both:	lives in Australia—can't speak Hindi
learns Hindi and French at school	are 12 years old, in final year of primary school	doesn't do a second language at school—does computers
lives in old, 3-bedroom house with big garden—no pets	do similar subjects at school	lives in modern, 4-bedroom house near beach—has Maltese poodles
goes to extra maths tuition—plays violin—plays soccer and basketball for school—does yoga and art after school	are taught in English	plays netball for a club—is a nipper at local surf lifesaving club—does dancing (ballet, jazz, tap) 3 times a week
all her ancestors born in India	have a mother, father, older brother and younger sister	father from Ireland—mother's grandparents from England
wants to be a history teacher	want to be teachers one day	wants to be a dance teacher

Page 104

1 a, b, c, e
2 **Answers will vary. Suggestions:** Like Divya, I also play soccer and basketball. However, I also go to karate and tae kwo do once a week.
3 My ancestry is more like Hayley's than Divya's, except my mother's family comes from Ireland and my father's family comes from England.

Pages 105–106

Step 1

1 a Although the girls' way of life is different in many ways, they have some things in common.
  b Divya's school starts at 8:30 am and ends at 2:30 pm, while Hayley's school starts at 9 am and ends at 3 pm.
  c Both girls learn English at school, but Divya also learns Hindi.
2 however, also, similarly, in addition, in contrast
3 a Divya does not have a pet, whereas Hayley has two Maltese poodles named Bubbles and Popcorn.
  b Unlike Divya, who lives in an old, three-bedroom house, Hayley lives in a modern, four-bedroom house.

Step 2

1 There are five people in each girl's family—a father, mother and three children.
2 Divya speaks English and Hindi, one of the main languages in India, fluently.
3 Hayley, on the other hand, plays netball, does surf lifesaving and goes to dancing.
4 While Divya and Haley come from different parts of the world, they share a number of different experiences.
5 Hayley goes to dancing three times a week where she does ballet, jazz and tap.

Step 3

1 Although Divya and Hayley both live in houses, Hayley's is more modern.
2 Hayley and Divya both speak English, but Divya also speaks Hindi well.
3 Hayley's dad emigrated to Australia from Ireland, and her mum's great-grandparents emigrated to Australia from England.

Step 4

Suggestion: This comparison between Divya and Hayley's lives shows that although the girls come from different countries that have different customs and traditions, they nevertheless share a number of similar experiences.

Pages 107–108

Divya and Hayley come from different parts of the world. Divya lives in Delhi, India and Hayley lives on the Sunshine Coast in Australia. Although the girls' way of life is different in many ways, they also have some things in common.

One way in which the girls' lives are similar is that both are in their final year at primary school and both have recently turned twelve. They learn similar subjects at school and both are taught in English. However Hindi, one of India's main languages, is also an important subject at Divya's school. The number of hours the girls spend at school each day is also similar. Divya's school starts at 8:30 am and ends at 2:30 pm, while Hayley's school starts at 9 am and finishes at 3 pm. In addition, both girls spend about an hour each day doing homework.

Another similarity between the girls is that they both take part in a number of extra-curricular activities, although the types of activities they do are different. Divya does yoga and goes to violin lessons. She also plays soccer and basketball for her school. Hayley, on the other hand, plays netball for a club and is a nipper at her local surf lifesaving club. She also goes to dancing three times a week, where she does ballet, jazz and tap.

The girls' families are also similar in some ways. There are five people in each family—a father, mother and three children. Divya has an older brother and a younger sister, and so has Hayley. The homes they live in, however, are different. Divya's family lives in an old, three-bedroom house set in a large garden, while Hayley lives in a modern, four-bedroom house near the beach.

One of the most obvious differences between the two girls is in their ancestry. Divya's parents, grandparents and other ancestors were all born in India. In contrast, Hayley's father was born in Ireland and her mother's great-grandparents immigrated to Australia from England at the end of the 19th century.

Comparing Divya and Hayley's lives shows that although they live in different countries with different customs and traditions, they nevertheless share a number of similar experiences.

Word bank

Unit 1 Factual recounts—newspaper reports

Verbs that can be used in place of *said* in direct speech:

announced, commented, declared, stated, explained, added, continued, remarked, replied

Unit 2 Restaurant reviews

Adjectives that describe food and drink:

Descriptive:

chewy, chilled, cool, creamy, crisp, crunchy, dry, fizzy, freshly squeezed, ice-cold, tender, tough

Evaluative:

delicious, divine, heavenly, mouth-watering, refreshing, scrumptious, tasteless, tasty, unappealing

Descriptive verbs for cooking and serving food:

coat, smother
drizzle, scatter, sprinkle, trickle, splash
dust, dredge
garnish, decorate, dress
ladle, scoop, spoon

Unit 3 Descriptions—photographs

Similes:

The shadows were like pools of water on the road.
Hedges lined the road like long benches.
The road was as grey as slate.
The leaves shimmered like sequins.
The fir trees were as tall as towers.
The trees cast ghost-like shadows in the distance.
The stagnant water was as smelly as a pair of old shoes.
The large leaf was as wrinkly as an old man's skin.
The land before us was as wide as the ocean.
The stars sparkled like diamonds in the sky.

Metaphors:

The roads were narrow ribbons far below.
A blanket of fog covered the city.
The land was covered in a carpet of wild flowers.
The water was a boiling pot of waves.
The sun cast slanting arrows of light into the room.
The news was music to my ears.
The story is a journey through time.
He is a pillar of strength.
She has the weight of the world on her shoulders.
That plan is a recipe for disaster.

Personification:

The tall buildings stood proudly to attention.
The flame danced in the light breeze.
The mountain wore a cloak of green.
The rocky outcrop gazed out to sea.
The lights winked at us as we drove by.
The raindrops tiptoed across the roof.
The thirsty plants were begging for water.
The whole country is caught in winter's icy grip.
The old chair groaned when I sat down.
Time just keeps marching on.

Descriptive verbs:

avoid, dodge, sidestep, skirt
blow, puff, spout
carved, cut, etched
drift, bob, float, wander
look, gaze, peep, peer
mark, stain, smudge, smear
swirl, billow, twist

Unit 4 Expositions—editorials

Connectives that link ideas:

also	consequently	for example	for instance
furthermore	however	in addition	instead
moreover	otherwise	nevertheless	so
therefore	too		

Modal adverbs:

Expressing certainty:

definitely	certainly	clearly	firmly
strongly	surely	undoubtedly	absolutely

Expressing uncertainty:

maybe	perhaps	possibly	probably

Unit 5 Explanations

Conjunctions:

after	although	because	before
so	unless	until	when
whereas	while	yet	

Relative pronouns:

who	whom	whose	which	that

Scientific language related to electricity/electronics:

thermal panels	photovoltaic panels
solar panels	electrical circuit
electrons	turbines
rotors	generator

Unit 6 Narratives

Similes:
The child was as happy as a dog with a bone.
The bicycle's wheels were like two big eyes.
His helmet was as snug as a shell on his head.
A bruise like a dark purple flower formed on his arm.
Scratches covered his knees like little scribbles.
She was as nervous as a kitten.
Her legs were as wobbly as jelly.
She felt like a fish out of water in her new environment.
Dad's harsh words were like a thorn festering inside his flesh.

Metaphors:
A bruise blossomed on his leg.
The bicycle was a scary monster.
I looked out at a sea of strange faces.
Her world fell apart.
This was unknown territory, and she was the alien.
The knot in her stomach grew tighter.
Dad's words stung him.

Personification:
The bicycle stared at him.
The bicycle mocked him.
The bicycle challenged him to ride it.
The bicycle was obeying him.

Descriptive synonyms for common verbs:
feared: fretted, dreaded
fell: crashed, tumbled
hurried: dashed, raced, rushed
hurt: wounded, tormented, tortured
held: grasped, clutched, clenched
moved: prodded, spurred
saw: glimpsed, noticed, spotted
stood: leaned, lounged, slouched
shone: gleamed, glistened
shook: trembled, quivered
talked: mumbled, murmured

Unit 7 Poetry—free verse poems

Descriptive words and phrases:
angry, furious, livid
bobbed, bounced, rocked
crouching, cowering
crying, sobbing, weeping
feel, touch, caress
flapping, beating, threshing, flailing
grab, snatch, seize
jutting out, protruding, extending
in a horrible way, grotesquely, in a hideous way
puckered, wrinkled, rumpled
pull, haul, tug, drag, jerk
rage, seethe, rant
resting, nestling
speed, zoom, streak
thin, flimsy, fragile
throw, fling, flick

Alliteration:
boat bobbing
blood boiling
fins like flimsy fans
silver scales sparkling in the sunlight

Similes:
anger bubbling like a volcano about to erupt
anxiety tugging at her heart, like mice gnawing on rope
arms jutting out like wings
beads like tiny drops of blood
eyes as dark as pools
heart fluttering like a bird trapped in a cage
heart jumped like a startled rabbit
heart melting like ice touched by the sun's warmth
jealousy seeping through her heart like a poisonous liquid.
little hands as delicate as petals
shaking like a leaf

Unit 8 Biographies

Time connectives:

afterwards	during that time	finally	first
in those days	shortly afterwards	now	
soon	then	these days	
today	tomorrow	yesterday	

Evaluative language:
Positive evaluation: successful, well-educated, excellent
Negative evaluation: harsh, poor, quarrelsome

Unit 9 Compare and contrast texts

Conjunctions that compare and contrast:

although	both … and	but
even though	unless	whereas
while	yet	

Adverbs that compare and contrast:

also	however	similarly	too

Phrases that compare and contrast:

compared to	in contrast
on the one hand	on the other hand